BEGINNER'S GUIDE TO MICROPROCESSORS

To Josie, Thea, John and Piper—who have never known a time without microprocessors.

No. 995
$8.95

BEGINNER'S GUIDE TO MICROPROCESSORS
BY CHARLES M. GILMORE

TAB BOOKS
Blue Ridge Summit, Pa. 17214

FIRST EDITION

FIRST PRINTING—NOVEMBER 1977

Copyright © 1977 by TAB BOOKS

Printed in the United States
of America

Library of Congress Cataloging in Publication Data

Gilmore, Charles Minot, 1942 -
   Beginner's guide to microprocessors.

   Includes index.
   1. Microprocessors. I. Title.
QA76.5.G514   621.3819'53   77-20857
ISBN 0-8306-7995-2
ISBN 0-8306-6995-7 pbk.

Contents

Credits

Preparing an introductory microprocessor book requires inputs from many sources. Long conversations with Heath Company personnel involved in microprocessor development helped significantly. Thanks go to: Bill Hannah, Vice-President of Engineering; Tom Yeager, Chief Engineer of Computer Products; and Lou Frenzel, Director of Computer Products, each of whom contributed many ideas; and to Donna Seddon, who typed and retyped many versions of the manuscript. A special note of thanks goes to my wife Polly, who not only edited the entire manuscript many times, but also learned a sufficient amount about microprocessors to critique the manuscript.

Charles M. Gilmore

Microprocessor is a term which is rapidly becoming as common as *electronics*. Indeed, the subject can be as complex as electronics, yet the fundamentals of microprocessors are as easy to understand as elementary electronics, if not easier. With the rapid growth of microprocessors, elementary microprocessor knowledge is as useful and interesting as elementary knowledge of solid-state electronics was during the '60s and the first half of the '70s.

The microprocessor is not yet a commonplace item in consumer electronic products, but its time is not far off. Microprocessors or microprocessor-like devices presently appear in microwave ovens, TV games, common and special purpose hand-held calculators, turntables, scanners, and in automotive system controls. These applications are just the beginning. The microprocessor is inexpensive, and one microprocessor system may perform many different functions by simply changing its program. Low cost and programming flexibility make it a natural component for consumer electronic products. The future will bring microprocessor based TVs, hi fi systems, games, calendars, information systems and a host of yet to be thought of products.

Knowing how the microprocessor works will enable you to get the most out of them. Who knows? In the future you may be able to make a minor program modification to a microprocessor-based product and give it a previously un-thought of function.

There are many books on microprocessors and microcomputers. Therefore you might ask "Why one more?", or "What does this book offer that the others don't?". Two approaches taken in this book differentiate it from the others currently available.

First, this book is designed to introduce the microprocessor to the completely uninitiated. Little or no background in either digital or analog electronics is required to obtain a working knowledge of this new and exciting revolution in electronics technology.

Second, the book is organized so it may be read in its entirety with no previous knowledge of the subject. However, if you have a smattering of microprocessor knowledge, this book has been organized with a glossary/reference approach to enable easy review of those areas of microprocessor technology that are unfamiliar.

The two 8-bit microprocessors which are currently most popular with the home experimenter have been chosen for a hardware discussion. This certainly does not mean they are the only two available or will remain the most popular devices in the future. The concepts presented in these chapters and in the other chapters are applicable to virtually all of the presently available microprocessors and will be applicable to future microprocessors as they are introduced, barring any radical change in computer architectural principles. Such a change will warrant the publication of many new books in the computing field.

Although the title of this book suggests contents strictly concerned with microprocessors, the fundamentals are by no means so restricted. You will find the information is directly applicable to microcomputers as well. To a lesser degree you will be able to use this information in the area of minicomputers, and will even have gained a fundamental knowledge of the operation of giant computers such as the IBM 370.

Chapter 1

An Introduction to the Microprocessor

"What is a *microprocessor?*" you might ask. A microprocessor is a digital computer contained in one or two integrated circuits. Why did the semiconductor industry work so hard to do this? And why has the electronics world been "revolutionized" by building an integrated circuit digital computer? To answer these questions, we must look at the two paths leading to the development of the microprocessor.

DEVELOPMENT OF THE MICROPROCESSOR

Digital computer technology has been growing steadily since the '50s. We have learned how to make the digital computer a large, complex machine capable of processing more data than man has ever before thought possible. We have also learned how to build and use smaller, less expensive computers. These computers, known as *minicomputers*, have found their way into many applications. A few years ago these applications could not have supported the expense of the large digital computers.

When we look at what can be done with the digital computer, we see it is capable of just about anything. What the computer does is determined by what it is programmed to do. If we want, we could program the computer to be a digital clock, a TV game, or a sophisticated calculator. In fact, we can reprogram the computer to do things tomorrow we haven't even thought of today. But even using the lowest cost minicomputer for these purposes is too expensive, and so, in many cases, the job goes undone.

Another technology has also been growing steadily since the '50s. This is the semiconductor industry, and it has been growing by leaps and bounds. The '50s saw the development of the diode and the transistor. The '60s saw the integrated circuit developed from just a few transistors on a single silicon chip to many thousands of transistors, capable of performing many complicated tasks on the same size chip.

Today we have custom integrated circuits of all types. The many digital clocks and watches are all operated by complicated integrated circuits (ICs). The calculator industry has grown overnight, from the simplest of four-function calculators to very complex programmable scientific and financial machines. Each new calculator is the result of one further step in IC technology. One of the most recent additions to the consumer electronics market is the TV game. First offered only in black and white with a single game, the TV game is now available in color with a choice of two, three, or more games selected by a flick of a switch, a result of IC technology growing stronger and stronger.

From all of this, one idea (thought) stands out. If we only had a digital computer that was cheap enough, we would not be required to keep designing different specialized integrated circuits. We would just reprogram our cheap digital computer for our latest brainstorm, and there would be our new product.

The road to the microprocessor is now clear. If the microprocessor really is an integrated circuit digital computer, then all we need to do the next time we have a brilliant idea is write a new program for our microprocessor.

It is, then, these paths which have lead us to the development of the microprocessor. First, we know almost any job to be done can be programmed in a digital computer. Second, we know this digital computer must be as cheap to build as custom integrated circuits, which have been developed for this purpose in the past. Third, we must have the digital integrated circuit technology to build the integrated circuit digital computer.

In the early 1970s, our abilities in the area of digital computers and integrated circuits reached this capability. The first microprocessor was born. It did not meet all the goals. It was too expensive for many applications, especially those in the consumer market. It couldn't hold enough information to perform many of the tasks being handled by the minicomputers of the time, but it was here. In the course of the past few years, the microprocessor has changed. The prices have dropped from hundreds of dollars for a single microprocessor to the point where a microprocessor IC can be sold for under $5.00. As digital computers, microprocessors have become so sophisticated it is difficult to tell them apart from minicomputers.

We have now seen the digital computer, in the form of the microprocessor, take the place of the custom ICs in many applications. They are being used as the basis of calculators, to run TV games, to control automobile emissions, and even to run juke boxes and electronic organs.

The road which lead to the development of the microprocessor is also the best road to understand the microprocessor. Once the basics of digital computer operation are understood, the basics of the microprocessor are at hand. Fortunately, the basics of the digital computer are simple. We think of digital computers in terms of their final product, that is doing hundreds and thousands of steps so rapidly we can't follow them at that speed. This makes it difficult for us to realize we can understand their operation by choosing a simple example and "slowing it down" step by step for us to follow. Broken down into its simple components and actions, the digital computer is really very simple.

HOW BIG IS A MICROPROCESSOR?

Physically, all microprocessors are virtually the same size. They are built on a silicon integrated circuit, approximately one-tenth to two-tenths of an inch on a side. These integrated circuits are placed in a variety of plastic and ceramic packages. Some typical packages are shown in Fig. 1-1.

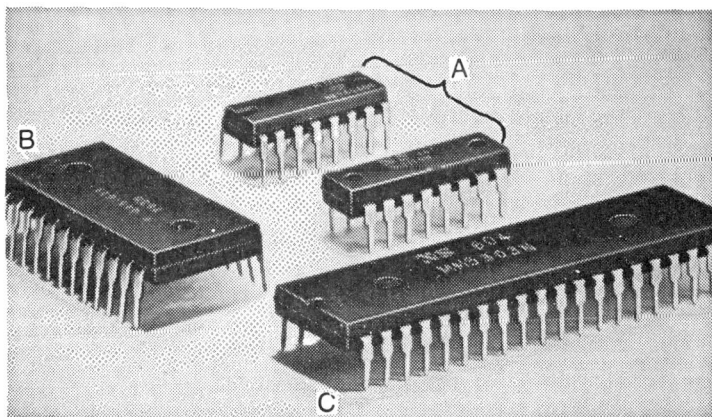

Fig. 1-1. Typical Dual-line Package (DIP) ICs commonly used for microprocessors and associated circuits. (A) 16-pin DIP (B) 24-pin DIP (C) 40-pin DIP.

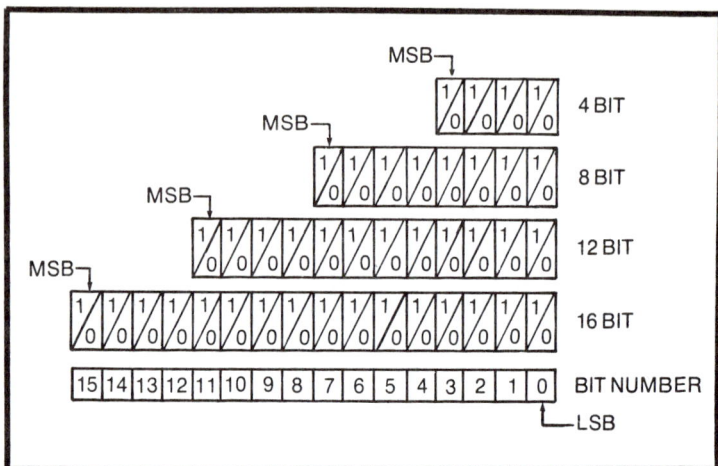

Fig. 1-2. Four-, eight-, twelve-, and sixteen-bit words. Note that each bit of the word may be either a one or a zero. Bits in a word are numbered from the Least Significant Bit (LSB), called bit 0, to the Most Significant Bit (MSB), which will be bit 3, bit 7, bit 11, or bit 15, depending on the word length.

The actual measure of microprocessor *size* is the length of the data words it operates on and the number of words its memory can store. For ease in handling and storage, data words in a microprocessor are all the same length. The *length* of the microprocessor word is measured by the number of bits per word. A *bit* is a binary dig*it*. Common microprocessor word lengths are 4, 8, 12, and 16 bits. Because the 8-bit data word is so common, it has been given the name *byte*. A byte is an 8-bit word.

The digital computer is *binary* in nature. There are only two possible conditions which may exist in a binary or digital circuit. They are either *on* or *off*. Therefore, there are only two possible conditions for each bit in a word. The bit may be either on or off. Commonly, the on/off conditions are referred to as "1" and "0". Figure 1-2 shows a number of different digital words. The difference between each of these words is its length. Each word has a *least significant bit* (LSB) and a *most significant bit* (MSB).

When thinking about the words in a digital computer we can relate to the simple calculator. For example, a simple 6-digit calculator always adds, subtracts, multiplies, or divides 6-digit numbers. If we are lucky, *leading* (*insignificant*) *zeroes* are suppressed. But in any case, the 6-digit calculator must always have a 6-digit number to work with. We cannot remove digits from the display or add them to the display. The microprocessor is the same way. If there are eight binary digits in its word, it must process eight digits at a time. No more, no less. The only difference between the eight bits of the digital computer and the eight digits of the calculator lies in the digits used. The bits in the computer may either be zero or one. In the calculator they may be anywhere from zero to nine.

If each bit may contain either a one or a zero, there are only two possible combinations which may exist for one bit. They are: one or zero. There are four possible combinations which may exist for two bits, they are: 00, 10, 01, and 11. The total number of combinations possible in a binary word in a given length is 2 raised to the Nth power. N is the number of bits in the word. Figure 1-3 shows the 16 possible combinations of ones and zeroes in a 4-bit word. This follows the formula 2 raised to the fourth power (2^4) equals 16 (e.g., $2 \times 2 \times 2 \times 2 = 16$). Although the first few powers of two are easily remembered, larger powers become difficult to remember. Appendix A gives a complete table of the powers of two used frequently in microprocessor operations.

As one measure of microprocessor size is the length of its word, this must also reflect on the microprocessor memory

COMBINATION	BIT 3	BIT 2	BIT 1	BIT 0
1	0	0	0	0
2	0	0	0	1
3	0	0	1	0
4	0	0	1	1
5	0	1	0	0
6	0	1	0	1
7	0	1	1	0
8	0	1	1	1
9	1	0	0	0
10	1	0	0	1
11	1	0	1	0
12	1	0	1	1
13	1	1	0	0
14	1	1	0	1
15	1	1	1	0
16	1	1	1	1

Fig. 1-3. The sixteen possible combinations of logical 1s and 0s in a single 4-bit digital word. Note that each combination is unique. The total combinations are given by the formula: combinations $= 2^4 = 16$. There are 256 combinations in an 8-bit word and 4096 in a 16-bit word.

size. The memory must be able to store a given number of words of this length. For example, a byte oriented microprocessor (an 8-bit microprocessor) is used with memory which can store 10 words. There are then 80 bits of storage capacity in the memory. Generally, we do not worry about the number of bits stored in the memory, but only the number of words. We assume, for example, a 4-bit microprocessor is accompanied by a memory capable of storing 4-bit words, and a 16-bit microprocessor has a memory with 16-bit words.

Memory size, then, is measured by the number of words it may store. Often the integrated circuit that we call a microprocessor contains little or no memory; the memory for these microprocessors is contained in other integrated circuits.

An integrated circuit package has a limited number of pins with which to make connections to other integrated circuits or anything else. Therefore, the number of connections between the microprocessor IC and the memory ICs must be kept to a minimum. To accomplish this, the connections which the microprocessor uses to address individual memory locations are in the form of *binary words*. The use of binary words makes much more efficient use of the connections. For example, if the memory only contained two words, two pins from the microprocessor could be used to address the desired word in memory. If word A was wanted, the pin corresponding to A could be activated. If the word B was wanted, the pin corresponding to word B could be activated. However, if the four possible binary combinations are used on pins A and B, that is 00, 10, 01, and 11, up to four memory words can be selected by these two pins. Following our earlier example, one can see up to 16 words can be selected using 4 pins.

Because binary words are used for addressing, the number of memory words associated with a particular microprocessor is usually a power of 2. For example, 1024 (2^{10}) is the closest power of 2 to 1000. For this reason, a 1K (nominally 1000 word) memory stores 1024 words. Very small microprocessor systems (a microprocessor system is a microprocessor, its associated memory, ICs, and other required circuitry) may only use 128, 256, or 512 words of memory. Larger microprocessor systems use 1K, 2K, 4K, 8K, 16K, 32K, or 65K words of memory, the actual number of words being rounded off to the nearest thousand for ease of reference.

Almost all microprocessor ICs have the capability of addressing large amounts of memory. However, as noted above, small microprocessor systems do not utilize anywhere near their memory capability, whereas large microprocessor systems may use one-half or the full amount of addressable memory.

BASIC COMPUTER OPERATION

The operation of a digital computer can be easily understood by thinking of the procedures used to play a simple child's game (Uncle Wiggly, for example). In this game, the player draws a white card with an instruction. Someone, of course, keeps track of exactly whose turn it is and which card is to be drawn next. The instruction is read, and the playing pieces are moved according to the instruction. Once the play has been made, the next instruction card in sequence is drawn from the deck. The game may not be quite that simple. Some cards change the regular drawing instruction card sequence. For example, the instruction *draw a card from the red deck* results in a change from the usual white-card sequence to a temporary red-card sequence. Other complications can occur as the playing piece moves a certain number of counts. As this happens, the instruction sequence may also change, and the player may miss a turn.

Let's now go through the rules for playing this game, but thinking of the instruction cards as a program stored in a computer memory. The player can be thought of as a digital circuit used to interpret instructions. This is called the Central Processing Unit (CPU). The playing pieces are the data being processed, as well as being moved in and out of memory. After the normal words for the game rules, equivalent computer terms for these operations follow in parenthesis.

In the game, the player (CPU) draws (FETCHES) a white card (WORD from MEMORY) with an instruction. Someone, of course, keeps track of exactly whose turn it is and which card is to be drawn next (THE PROGRAM COUNTER). The instruction is read (interpreted by the CPU), and the playing pieces (DATA) are moved (PROCESSED) according to the instruction. Once the play has been made (EXECUTED), the next instruction card in sequence (WORD) is drawn (FETCHED) from the deck (MEMORY). The game may not be quite that simple. Some cards (INSTRUCTION WORDS) change the regular drawing instruction card drawing sequence. For example, the instruction *draw a card from the red deck* (GO DO A SUBROUTINE) results in a change from the usual white card sequence to a temporary red card sequence (FINISH THE SUBROUTINE BEFORE

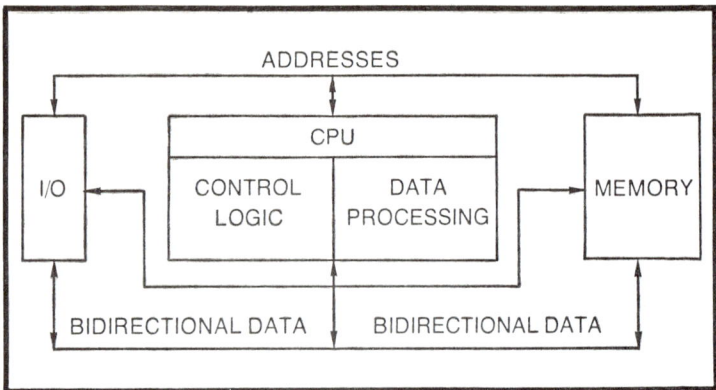

Fig. 1-4. A simple block diagram of a microcomputer or microprocessor. The microprocessor may contain both the CPU and the memory, or it may contain the memory alone. Occasionally I/O drivers may be contained within the microprocessor.

FETCHING WORDS FROM THE PROGRAM IN A REGULAR SEQUENCE). Other complications can occur as the playing piece moves a certain number of counts (PROCESSING THE DATA to a certain predetermined point). As this happens, the instruction sequence may also change and the player may miss a turn (a *skip* or *jump* is caused and the computer must wait for a FETCH/EXECUTE cycle before proceeding or starts the FETCH/EXECUTE sequence in a new place in the deck).

Keeping the simple operations of the child's game in mind, we can examine the internal parts of a microprocessor in more detail.

In simple form, the microprocessor system consists of three parts. They are the CPU, the memory, and the I/O (input and output) devices. A microprocessor always contains the CPU. Some microprocessors contain a CPU and memory. A few microprocessors have a CPU, memory, and some form of I/O capability. Figure 1-4 shows this in a simplified diagram. Note that data (words which represent numbers) flows to and from the CPU and either the memory or I/O. The CPU has the ability to send *address* information to either the memory or the I/O device. The address information tells the memory which word is being FETCHED as an instruction, or what location the data is to be stored in or retrieved from.

Everything the computer does is a version of this simple FETCH/EXECUTE cycle used in the game.

Just as the memory must have an address before data may be transferred to or from it, so must an I/O device.

Normally there is more than one input device or output device on the system. Therefore, the CPU must decide which one it wishes to transfer data with. It tells that device it wishes to transfer data with it by addressing it.

We have discussed removing the instruction words from memory and transferring data words to and from memory. This implies there is no difference between data and instruction words and that either may be located anywhere in memory. Indeed this is the case. In fact, this is just one more demonstration of the versatility of the digital computer. To execute a particular program, the programmer may set aside certain areas of memory for program storage. Other areas of memory may be set aside for data storage. These assignments may change for a different program *if* the programmer wishes. The only requirement is (like the instruction cards in the game) the instruction words making up the computer program must be stored in the sequence in which they are to be used.

We now take a more detailed look at each of the major sections making up a microprocessor based system. The CPU is covered first, as it is really the brains of the computer. Memory and I/O devices are covered in following chapters. Understanding each of these portions of the microprocessor system is important to understanding microprocessors.

As we have noted before, the term microprocessor does not exactly define its contents. All microprocessors have a CPU. Many contain CPU and memory, and some contain CPU memory and I/O connections (called *ports*). Obviously, understanding what makes up the CPU and how the CPU operates is vital to understanding the microprocessor. The terms CPU and microprocessor are occasionally used interchangeably. Although this is a bit careless, it is not entirely inaccurate, for all microprocessors do have a CPU, and in many cases, the microprocessor is the microprocessor system or the microcomputer's CPU. To restate this in another way, a microprocessor may be used as a CPU for a small digital computer called a microcomputer. The difference between microcomputers and minicomputers usually indicates the CPU is a microprocessor rather than being built with many individual digital integrated circuits.

WHERE TO GO FROM HERE

How you will use this book depends on just how much you already know about digital electronics and microprocessors. It is important to realize you can learn a good deal about microprocessors without having to learn anything about electronics or electricity. If you plan to do more than just learn a little about microprocessors and experiment with them, you will need some basic electronics knowledge. However, this need be far less than if you had decided to learn about hi-fi or ham radio, for example.

Following this chapter is a glossary of terms. The glossary is followed by individual chapters covering many of the separate topics concerning microprocessors in more detail. If you feel like plowing ahead, move to those chapters which are of the greatest interest to you. If you come across a term you are not familiar with, refer to the glossary. If the glossary is not detailed enough, each definition is followed by a text reference where the term is covered in detail.

If you have never read anything on digital electronics, start with the chapter on digital logic (immediately following the glossary) and proceed from there. Once again, if there are terms which you know you have read in earlier chapters but have since become hazy about, use the glossary.

Chapter 2

Glossary of Microprocessor Terms

The following glossary of microprocessor terms provides a short definition of many of the terms used throughout this book. Each term in the glossary is expanded at appropriate points in the book itself.

absolute address   The actual binary address of a memory location contained in a memory-reference instruction.

access time   The time between when data is called for and when it is delivered.

accumulator   The main CPU register where results of arithmetic and logical operations are stored. Some microprocessors have two accumulators or have multiple registers which serve as accumulators.

adder   A logic circuit that is a combination of gates wired to perform binary addition of two input-signals. A full adder usually includes a carry input, and a sum and carry output.

address   The binary number pointing to (identifying) a memory location (or an input/output port). Addressing is usually accomplished by a 12- or 16-bit binary number. This number may be converted into an octal or hexidecimal number.

address decoder   A logic circuit whose output selects a single addressed device, addressed by a binary number. The binary number is a decoder input.

algorithm   A set of rules (usually mathematical) to solve a particular problem.

ALU (Arithmetic Logic Unit) A logic circuit performing arithmetic and logical functions on data words. ALUs provide microprocessors with such functions as add, subtract, shift, increment, decrement, AND, OR, and EXCLUSIVE OR.

architecture The internal organization of a microprocessor. The interconnections of registers, ALUs, control logic, etc. That which makes one microprocessor different from another.

ASCII (American Standard Code for Information Interchange) ASCII is an eight-level code for serial transmission of alphanumerical data. The first 7 bits represent 128 standard ASCII characters (see Appendix B). The eighth data bit is a parity bit for error checking. The eight data bits are preceded by one start bit and followed by one or two stop bits.

assembler A programming language which converts mnemonics (symbol code or abbreviations for machine opcodes) into machine code. Assemblers allow the programmer to use names (labels) rather than numerical values for addressed locations. The assembler converts labels into absolute addresses.

asynchronous Serial communications, e.g. words, having no regular time interval between transmitted or received words. The start bit of each word synchronizes the reading of the individual word.

BASIC A conversational programming language originally developed by Dartmouth College. This language permits the use of simple English words and common mathematical symbols to perform the necessary arithmetic and logical operations to solve the problems. BASIC is an interpretive language.

baud rate The data transmission rate. For an asynchronous word this is the data rate of the individual bits within the single word.

bidirectional Data lines used to send and receive data. Signals flow in both directions on a bidirectional data bus.

binary number system A number system expressing quantities using only the symbols 1 and 0. Digital logic uses binary signals.

bipolar Conventional transistor construction using both positive- and negative-doped semiconductor materials (both PNP and NPN transistors).

bit A binary digit. The smallest unit of data in a digital system or microprocessor.

bus   A digital communications path between a micro-processor and other associated devices. The bus generally carries bidirectional data or unidirectional address information. Buses normally have 4, 8, 12, or 16 parallel lines each carrying 1 bit of a 4, 8, 12, or 16 bit word.

byte   A digital number consisting of eight bits.

carry   An arithmetic overflow. In microprocessors this overflow is greater than the word size permits.

chip   A small silicon square used to build an integrated circuit. Often this term is used interchangeably with integrated circuit.

clock   A pulse generator giving the microprocessor, memory, and I/O devices common timing signals. Clocks are usually single phase or two phase (1ϕ or 2ϕ).

code   A series of characters and symbols which represent programming instructions for a microprocessor. A method for expressing a program.

combinational logic   Digital circuits created by combining gates to perform a required function. Combinational logic circuits do not have storage capabilities.

compiler   The program which reduces a logical solution of a problem expressed in English statements and ordinary algebra to a series of machine code instructions for a specific microprocessor.

complement   To invert a logic signal. That is, to make a logic 0 from a logic 1 and vice versa.

CMOS (Complementary Metal Oxide Semiconductor)   An extremely low-power MOS technology used to build some microprocessors and memories.

console   The operating panel or terminal for a microprocessor system.

CPU (Central Processing Unit)   All the microprocessor logic, including registers, ALU, timing, and control circuitry.

crash   Complete loss of microprocessor control. A microprocessor usually crashes when the wrong sequence of instructions is processed.

CROM (Control Read Only Memory)   Internal memory in a microprocessor used to implement control sequences.

cross assembler   A program producing binary code from assembler source code suitable for a particular microprocessor. The cross assembler is run on a different or *host* computer.

CRT (Cathode Ray Tube) This term usually refers to a terminal which employs a television-like screen for readout rather than a printer.

data A number of binary words containing information which has been or is to be processed by the microprocessor.

debug routine A short program which permits the microprocessor programmer to analyze and correct programs stored in memory. The programmer works directly in machine code, usually expressed in octal or hexidecimal.

decoder A logic circuit which selects one of N outputs based on a parallel binary input. Example, a four-line to one-of-16-line decoder.

decrement To decrease the value of a counter by one, or more if so specified.

device A term referring to transistors or to equipment connected to a microprocessor system.

diagnostic programs Programs designed to test certain portions of the microprocessor system, assuring proper operation.

DIP (Dual In-line Package) A ceramic or plastic package commonly used for integrated circuits.

disc A high speed mass storage device for program and data information. The information is stored on a rotating circular disc coated with a magnetic material similar to magnetic recording tape. Data is written and read by fixed or movable heads positioned over the disc.

DMA (Direct Memory Access) A special operation where the microprocessor gives up control of the memory and allows an external device to read or write into large blocks of memory.

double precision arithmetic Arithmetic operations performed using two successive accumulator operations.

dynamic An MOS construction technique using charged capacitors to hold digital information. Dynamic devices must be refreshed to prevent information loss due to charge leakage.

ECL (Emitter Coupled Logic) A high speed logic using bipolar technology. ECL is the fastest logic in use today. Its primary use is the construction of very high speed memories and specialized microprocessors.

editor A program which allows the programmer to write and modify source code using the microprocessor and a terminal as a very sophisticated typewriter.

enable A signal permitting a logic circuit to carry out its intended function.

EPROM (Erasible Programmable Read Only Memory) A read-only memory which can be erased either by an electrical signal or by ultraviolet light.

execute Portion of a microprocessor cycle where the instructions fetched from memory are carried out.

fetch Reading the next program step from memory and storing it in the instruction register.

file A collection of data in microprocessor memory or mass storage all pertaining to a single subject.

flag A single storage bit indicating a certain condition exists (or existed).

flip-flop A logic circuit having two stable states which may be set or reset upon command.

floppy disc A rotating mass storage device using an 8-inch diameter piece of magnetic tape. Floppy discs typically hold 256,000 bytes.

flow chart A graphical method of representing a sequence of program steps to be performed by a microprocessor.

FORTRAN (FORmula TRANslator) A science-oriented high level language. Usually a compiler.

gate A logic circuit with two or more inputs and a single output whose state is defined by the combination of logic 1s and 0s at the inputs.

halt Causing the microprocessor to stop the fetch/execute cycle. Halting the microprocessor does not necessarily mean shutting off the clock.

hard copy Printed output from a microprocessor as opposed to the information displayed on a CRT or on LEDs.

hardware A generalized term referring to the electronic circuits, printed circuit boards, chassis, etc., involved in the microprocessor.

hexidecimal A number system involving 16 characters; usually the characters, 0, 1, 2, 3, 4, 5, 6, 7, 8, 9, A, B, C, D, E, F, are used. Hexidecimal is frequently used as shorthand notation to represent the 4-bit binary numbers 0000 to 1111.

hi-byte The most significant eight bits of a multiple byte word.

high level language A computer language using English words, decimal arithmetic, and common algebraic expressions. Each line or statement represents a large number of computer operations.

increment To increase the value of a counter by one, or more if so specified.

index register A CPU register containing a reference number. When a second number is subtracted from the index register a memory address is given.

indirect addressing A form of double-step addressing. That is, the first memory location or register addressed does not contain the desired information but rather contains the address of the register or memory location of the desired information.

instruction set A list of the operations which a microprocessor performs in response to a given binary code.

interface The circuits necessary to connect the microprocessor to some given device. The device may be memory or input/output devices. Interfacing is a general term for interconnecting electronic devices.

interpreter A program which solves a problem on a step-by-step basis, rather than converting the problem to machine language in its entirety prior to processing.

interrupt A microprocessor input line signaling an external device must be serviced. Interrupt causes the microprocessor to complete the current instruction cycle, then service the external device.

I/O (Input/Output) Generalized terms referring to any device (except memory) which supplies information to the microprocessor or which the microprocessor supplies information to.

instruction register The register within the microprocessor which receives the program word and stores it while the program word is decoded and executed.

IC (Integrated Circuit) An electronic circuit built on a single silicon wafer containing many transistors interconnected to perform a specific function. ICs come in three sizes: SSI (Small Scale Integration <20 gates); MSI (Medium Scale Integration 20−200 gates); and LSI (Large Scale Integration >200 gates). Microprocessors are LSI.

jump An instruction which causes a program counter to start at a new location. Jumps may be unconditional or conditional.

level From ASCII, as in eight level.

link A single-bit register containing information about arithmetic overflows from a previous accumulator activity.

loader A short program used to read specially prepared binary information into sequential memory locations. Loaders contain error detection subroutines and methods to change the load point in memory.

loop A programming technique which continually returns the microprocessor to the same instruction until a specific condition is reached.

lo-byte The least significant eight bits of a multiple byte word.

LSB (Least Significant Bit) The bit having the lowest weight (least significance) on the value of a binary word.

machine instruction Microprocessor instructions expressed in their binary form.

machine language program A program consisting of a series of machine instructions written in binary, octal, or hexidecimal notation.

mass storage Storage external to the main microprocessor memory generally capable of holding many times the capacity of the main microprocessor memory.

memory The circuits in which microprocessor data and instructions are stored.

microcomputer An entire computer system built using a microprocessor as the central processing unit.

microprocessor An integrated circuit (usually large scale integration) which performs all the functions normally found in a digital computer central processing unit.

microprogramming The circuit implementation for decoding and carrying out fetched instruction. A microprogrammed microprocessor usually looks up the instructions in a CROM.

mnemonics English abbreviations which have a one for one correlation to a microprocessor instruction set. Mnemonic code can be converted into binary instructions by the programmer. This is called *hand assembly*. A program which converts mnemonic machine code is an *assembler*.

monitor A program which oversees the operation, handling, and timing of a number of other programs.

MOS (Metal Oxide Semiconductor) A semiconductor technology with low power consumption. Generally used to fabricate LSI circuits such as microprocessors, memories, and communications devices.

MSB (Most Significant Bit) The bit in a binary word which when changed has the greatest effect upon the value of the word.

multiplexer A logic circuit which upon command connects one selected input from a number of inputs to a single output.

octal A number system using the symbols 0, 1, 2, 3, 4, 5, 6, 7. Octal numbers are frequently used as a shorthand notation to represent the 3-bit binary numbers 000 to 111.

opcode (operation code) A portion of a computer instruction word designating the basic function performed by the instruction.

parallel Moving a digital word from one place to another where all bits are moved simultaneously.

parity Adding an extra bit to a binary number for checking accuracy.

peripheral A device such as a printer or mass storage unit which is an accessory to a microprocessor or microcomputer.

polling A programming technique which tests one or more I/O devices in sequence for a designated condition.

processor A central portion of a computer synonymous with CPU.

program counter A register in the CPU which indicates the memory address of the next instruction.

programming Writing a sequence of computer instructions to solve a specific problem, or to perform a specific task.

PROM (Programmable Read Only Memory A memory device which may be programmed by someone other than the integrated circuit manufacturer. Programming of the memory can be done only once with special programming equipment.

push/pop Placing information onto a stack or removing information from a stack.

RAM (Random Access Memory) Any read/write memory whose cells can be randomly accessed by a parallel binary address word rather than sequentially accessed in time.

read Retrieving data from a memory or I/O location.

ROM (Read Only Memory) A memory device which contains a permanent set of digital words. ROMs may not be rewritten.

register A logic circuit to store a single binary word.

relative addressing An addressing technique where the addressed word is found by adding a number to or subtracting a number from the program counter value.

return A microprocessor instruction which directs the microprocessor to pop a value from the stack into the program counter, returning the program counter to the sequence of an original program ending a subroutine.

rotate A shift register operation where the shift register output is connected to its own input, so no information is lost.

run A condition when the microprocessor is sequentially fetching and executing instructions.

sequential logic Logic circuits using one or more flip-flops. The present output rates of sequential logic circuits are not only a function of current inputs, but also of previous inputs.

serial A method of transmitting data words one bit at a time, rather than transmitting the entire word over multiple lines.

single-phase clock An oscillator which supplies a single square wave as timing signals for a microprocessor.

software All the programs and programming information supporting a microprocessor.

source program A written set of directions defining the logical solutions to a problem. A source program must be translated to machine code by a second secondary program such as an assembler, compiler, or an interpreter before the computer can solve the program.

stack A series of registers or memory locations where the program counter contents may be placed for temporary storage.

status register A CPU register indicating the condition caused by the last arithmetic or logic register operation. Status registers normally indicate, at least, zero conditions, arithmetic overflows, and negative conditions.

stored program The basic technique by which a microprocessor carries out a sequence of operations to solve a particular problem. The instructions are stored in the microprocessor's memory.

subroutine A short program performing a specific function, frequently used by many portions of the program or by many different programs.

switch register A group of switches (usually 8 or 16) which can be addressed by the CPU to manually input information into CPU registers or memory.

teleprinter A console terminal device which prints on rolled 8 1/2 inch wide paper, and has a full ASCII keyboard. Teleprinters usually communicate with microprocessors via a serial ASCII 20 mA loop for transmit and a serial ASCII 20 mA loop for receive.

tristate A neutral condition at a logic element output. When the logic element is in the tristate condition, the output is neither a logic 1 nor a logic 0. The output may be wired in parallel with other outputs, which may be in the tristate condition or may be supplying a logic 1 or logic 0. The tristate condition disconnects a particular logic element from its output.

truth table A form showing all possible input conditions and the resulting output conditions for a logic circuit.

TTL (Transistor Traistor Logic) A common form of logic construction used for small scale and medium scale integration.

two-phase clock An oscillator which supplies two nonoverlapping square waves as timing signals for the microprocessor.

UART (Universal Asychronous Receiver Transmitter) An LSI circuit which converts parallel inputs to serial data, adding required start and stop bits. It also converts serial data, including start and stop bits, to parallel words. UARTs usually also perform some error detecting functions.

vectored interrupt An interrupt which directs the microprocessor to start a service routine at particular address (vector).

volatile A term describing memory which does not retain its contents when power is lost.

word A fixed number of bits associated with a particular microprocessor. An 8-bit word is frequently called a byte.

write Transferring data to memory or to an output port.

Chapter 3

Binary Arithmetic

In order to use the microprocessor you must be able to program it. In order to program the microprocessor you must understand the basics of binary arithmetic. The microprocessor cannot add, subtract, multiply, or divide the decimal numbers we are accustomed to. The microprocessor works in the world of ones and zeros. This is called binary arithmetic. Binary arithmetic is capable of performing all the functions used in decimal arithmetic. That is, there is binary addition, binary subtraction, binary multiplication, and binary division. In addition, decimal numbers entered on a keyboard or a teleprinter, for example, can be converted to binary numbers. The microprocessor can manipulate these binary numbers and convert the binary results into decimal numbers for printing or display.

BINARY, OCTAL, AND HEXIDECIMAL NUMBER SYSTEMS

How do binary numbers relate to decimal numbers? There are only two digits in the binary system, one and zero. These are usually equated to the electrical signals on and off. The primary function of a number system is to count. The number indicates the quantity being measured. That is, if there are three of an object, we use a symbol that is the Arabic numeral for three. What is used in the binary system? If there is nothing, a zero (0) is the logical symbol. If there is one thing, the symbol one (1) is used. This is the entire stock of binary digits. To continue increasing, we must do what the decimal system does after counting exceeds the symbol nine. That is,

DECIMAL	BINARY	OCTAL	HEX
34	100010	42	22
63	111111	77	3F
64	1000000	100	40
127	1111111	177	7F
128	10000000	200	80
255	11111111	377	FF
256	100000000	400	100

Fig. 3-1. Decimal, binary, octal, and hexidecimal numbers. Note that all numbers are shown with their leading zeros suppressed. For example, decimal 32 could be written 032, as binary four (100) could be written 0100.

repeat in an additional column. Two is represented by two columns of binary digits; the symbol is 10. Three is represented by the symbol 11. Once again, all possible combinations have been used. Therefore we move to a third column and begin the sequence at four (100), five (101), six (110), and seven (111). Once again, we are out of possible combinations, and we must move to a fourth column. An extension of this increasing of the number of columns in basic binary counting is shown in Fig. 3-1.

As you can see, counting is done using only two symbols (0 and 1), instead of the familiar ten (0, 1, 2, 3, 4, 5, 6, 7, 8, and 9). Another way of saying this is to say we are counting in base two for the binary column. Obviously, decimal is counting in base ten. There are other number systems used. We can count in base eight, where the symbols are 0, 1, 2, 3, 4, 5, 6, and 7. This is called octal. Some octal numbers are shown in the third column of Table 3-1. The fourth column shows hexidecimal (hex) numbers. The hexidecimal system uses 16 different symbols before repeating. The hexidecimal number system is a base 16 number system. Hexidecimal numbering uses the symbols 0, 1, 2, 3, 4, 5, 6, 7, 8, 9, A, B, C, D, E, and F. Table 3-1 lists all these systems for decimal numbers 0 through 33.

Why use base 8 and base 16 number systems in microprocessors when only two number-systems seem to be needed? The need for binary is easy to understand because microprocessors are digital in nature and digital systems make use of a two-symbol number system. Of course, decimal is obvious because we have been taught decimal arithmetic since early childhood, and this is the number system we are familiar with. Octal and hexidecimal are used in the microprocessor world because they are simpler, more easily remembered ways to represent binary numbers.

For example, referring to Fig. 3-2, see the binary number 11101011 at A. This is the binary representation of the decimal number 235. The binary equivalent of 235 may be an instruction for a microprocessor, or data stored in memory. However, no matter what it is, it consists of 8 digits and it is long and difficult to remember. The conversion process from binary to decimal is easy to remember but is cumbersome, as is the conversion process from decimal to binary. However, conversion from binary to octal or binary to hexidecimal is really quite simple. The reason for this simplicity is that binary octal and hexidecimal number systems each have a base which is a power of 2. The base of the decimal system (10) is not a power of 2.

Breaking the binary number into groups of threes, starting with the least significant bit, separates the number as shown in Fig. 3-2B. The most significant zero is added to make even

Table 3-1. Comparisons of Common Number Systems.

DECIMAL	BINARY	OCTAL	HEX
0	0	0	0
1	1	1	1
2	10	2	2
3	11	3	3
4	100	4	4
5	101	5	5
6	110	6	6
7	111	7	7
8	1000	10	8
9	1001	11	9
10	1010	12	A
11	1011	13	B
12	1100	14	C
13	1101	15	D
14	1110	16	E
15	1111	17	F
16	10000	20	10
17	10001	21	11
18	10010	22	12
19	10011	23	13
20	10100	24	14
21	10101	25	15
22	10110	26	16
23	10111	27	17
24	11000	30	18
25	11001	31	19
26	11010	32	1A
27	11011	33	1B
28	11100	34	1C
29	11101	35	1D
30	11110	36	1E
31	11111	37	1F
32	100000	40	20
33	100001	41	21

11101011	A. The eight-bit binary representation of the decimal number 235
011 101 011	B. Breaking the eight-bit number into groups of three. Note that an insignificant zero is added to make complete groups of three bits
011 101 011 binary 3 5 3 = 353_8	C. Expressing the binary number as an OCTAL number
1110 1011 E B = EB_{16}	D. Breaking the binary number into two groups of four bits to generate a two-digit hex number.

Fig. 3-2. Comparisons of decimal, binary, octal and hexidecimal numbers.

groups of threes. From Table 3-1 one can look up the octal equivalent for each three bit binary number. The octal equivalent of 011 is 3, the octal equivalent of 101 is 5, and the octal equivalent of 011 is 3.

We therefore may express this binary number as 353 base 8, as shown in Fig. 3-2C. The base 8 is shown by the subscripted 8 at the end of the number. Another way of saying this is that decimal 235 is 353 when converted to octal.

To convert octal 353 back to binary, all we must know is the equivalence between each octal digit and its three binary combinations. For example, the octal number 267 may be converted to the binary as follows:

1. The binary equivalent of 7 is 111;
2. The binary equivalent of 6 is 110; and
3. The binary equivalent of 2 is 010.

Therefore, 267_8 is one method of representing the binary number 10110111. Note in significant zeroes, the most significant bits are dropped as is customary in all number systems. For example, we do not write decimal 10 as 00010, but simply as 10.

Again, referring to the example in Fig. 3-2, we may wish to use hexidecimal representation rather than octal. Hexidecimal representation has the advantage that the binary number is broken into groups of four bits each. When working with 8-bit or 16-bit binary numbers, this is particularly convenient. Referring to Fig. 3-2D the binary number 11101011 breaks into two groups of four binary digits each. The most significant group is 1110 and the least significant group is 1011. Looking at Table 3-1 once again, we can find the equivalent hexidecimal symbol for each group of four binary digits. The group 1011 converts to the hexidecimal symbol B, and the most significant 4-bit binary group 1110 converts to the hexidecimal symbol E. This results in the hexidecimal number EB. Note, hexidecimal numbers are a mixture of what we think of as numerals and letters. However, the numerals 0 through 9 and the letters A through F are all treated as individual numerals in hexidecimal.

Converting from hexidecimal to binary is equally simple. For example, converting the hexidecimal number 6F into binary is accomplished by looking up the 4-bit equivalence of 6 and F. Again, looking in Table 3-1, we find the binary equivalent of F is 1111 and the binary equivalent of 6 is 0110. Therefore, the 8-bit binary number represented by the two-digit hexidecimal number 6F is 01101111.

Both octal and hexidecimal are commonly used in microprocessor work. Each has its own advantages. Octal is perhaps somewhat easier to remember. There are only 8 total characters and therefore only eight 3-bit binary combinations which must be remembered. On the other hand, most microprocessors are of 4-, 8-, or 16-bits. These do not conveniently break into groups of threes. We must add insignificant leading zeroes to the binary numbers to create groups of three. One combination does readily break into groups of threes. This is the 12-bit binary number used on one major minicomputer, Digital Equipment Corporation's PDP-8. Hexidecimal offers the advantage of readily breaking into groups of four, which easily matches 4-bit, 8-bit, and 16-bit microprocessors. However, if you use hexidecimal you must remember 16, not 8 combinations of 4-bit binary numbers.

BINARY TO DECIMAL AND
DECIMAL TO BINARY CONVERSIONS

How do we convert from binary numbers to their decimal equivalent and from decimal numbers to the equivalent binary number? There are a number of *algorithms* (mathematical routines) for making these conversions. One of the two presented here is simple and may be done either by the microprocessor or by paper and pencil. If desired, more sophisticated algorithms may be utilized which do not use as much memory.

When converting from binary to decimal, each place in the binary number is assigned a decimal weight, just as each place in a decimal number is assigned a decimal weight. That is, when we look at the decimal number 1,246 we say the 6 is in the units place, the 4 is in the tens place, the 2 is in the hundreds place, and the 1 is in the thousands place. Binary places are assigned a decimal weight which is a power of two. For example, in an 8-bit binary number the first place is 2^0 or 1. The second place is 2^1 or 2, the third place is 2^2 or 4, the fourth place is 2^3 or 8, the fifth place is 2^4 or 16, the sixth place is 2^5 or 32, the seventh place is 2^6 or 64, and the eighth place is 2^7 power of 128. If a one exists in any place, add the weight of that place to the total. If a zero exists in the place, skip the weight in that place. For example, earlier, we used the binary number 11101011. Assigning decimal weights to each place given:

2^7	2^6	2^5	2^4	2^3	2^2	2^1	2^0
(128)	(64)	(32)	(16)	(8)	(4)	(2)	(1)

$$128 + 64 + 32 + 0 + 8 + 0 + 2 + 1 = 235$$

Obviously, this may be extended to more than eight columns, if there are more than eight bits in the binary number. Simply reversing this process converts decimal to binary. First, we assign weighted places not knowing whether the place is to contain a 1 or a 0. Ones and zeros are filled in so the total yields the desired decimal number.

For example, to convert the decimal number 132 to the equivalent 8-bit binary number we may use the following sequence:

1. A 1 is placed under the 128. As the total does not exceed 132, the 1 is left.
2. A 1 is placed under the 64, but 64 + 128 exceeds 132, so the 1 is removed and replaced with a 0.
3. A 1 is placed under the 32, but 128 + 32 exceeds 132, so the 1 is removed and replaced with a 0.
4. A 1 is placed under the 16, but 128 + 16 exceeds 132, so the 1 is removed and replaced with a 0.
5. A 1 is placed under the 8, but the 128 + 8 exceeds 132, so the 1 is removed and replaced with a 0.
6. A 1 is placed under the 4; as the total does not exceed 132, the 1 is left.
7. A 1 is placed under the 2, but 128 + 4 + 2 exceeds 132; therefore, the 1 is removed and replaced with a 0.
8. A 1 is placed under the 1, but 128 + 4 + 1 exceeds 132; therefore, the 1 is removed and replaced with a 0.

We are left, therefore, with the binary number 10000100. This procedure may be extended to more bits, if the number exceeds 255, the total achieved in an 8-bit number when all bits are 1. Fewer bits may also be used if small numbers are involved.

As you can see, decimal numbers can easily exceed the number which may be represented by a single word in an 8-bit microprocessor. When this condition exists, the decimal number may be represented by two, three, or even four 8-bit numbers within the microprocessor. For example, two 8-bit numbers give a range of 0 to 131,071. This technique is called *double precision*. Using three 8-bit binary numbers allows the use of numbers between 0 and 33,554,431. This, of course, allows greater than seven digits of precision in a decimal number.

The *most significant bit* of the binary number is used to represent positive and negative numbers. If the number is positive, the most significant bit is zero. If the number is negative, the most significant bit is one. This convention permits simple subtraction as will be seen later. Using this convention, which is called *two's complement* arithmetic, the number of bits or precision is reduced by one. That is, an 8-bit number contains a sign bit in the most significant position and seven bits of resolution. Therefore, an 8-bit number can represent decimal numbers lying between -127 and $+127$. Using double precision, we may represent numbers lying between $-65,535$ and $+65,535$. Triple precision using an 8-bit number means we have 1 sign bit and 23 data bits. This allows the range of numbers between $-16,077,215$ and $+16,077,215$. This is very commonly used because it is approximately seven decimal digits of accuracy.

BINARY ADDITION

Binary addition is relatively simple. As with any number system, there are basic rules to add numbers. These rules for binary addition are:

1. $0 + 0 = 0$
2. $1 + 0 = 1$
3. $0 + 1 = 1$
4. $1 + 1 = 0$ plus a carry of 1

If we wish to add two binary numbers, these simple rules apply. Figure 3-3 shows the addition of two 8-bit binary numbers, and the equivalent decimal addition. If the result

	DECIMAL	BINARY
Fig. 3-3. The addition of two 8-bit binary numbers.	65	01000001
	72	01001000
	137	10001001

| | | | | | 1 | ←— 1 Carry from first |

32768	16384	8192	4096	2048	1024	512	256		128	64	32	16	8	4	2	1
0	0	1	0	1	1	0	1		1	1	0	0	0	0	1	0
0	1	0	1	1	0	0	1		0	1	0	0	1	1	0	1
1	0	0	0	0	1	1	1		0	0	0	0	1	1	1	1

SECOND ADDITION   FIRST ADDITION

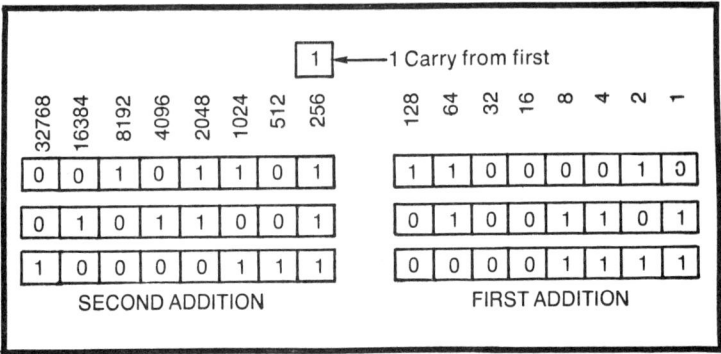

Fig. 3-4. A double-precision addition with a carry sign generated from the least significant addition. The carry bit is stored and used as an input to the second addition.

exceeds eight bits, a carry is generated. In the microprocessor the carry bit is stored. It is used as an input to the addition of two 8-bit numbers making up the most significant portion of the addition in double precision arithmetic. This is shown in Fig. 3-4.

BINARY SUBTRACTION

Binary subtraction may be accomplished in a number of different ways. One way is to have a simple set of rules such as those used for binary addition. If these rules are followed, two binary numbers may be subtracted. However, in order to properly accomplish subtraction, we must pay attention to the sign and magnitude of the numbers involved. If sign and magnitude are not watched, the sign of the result is in question. For example, if a small positive number is subtracted from a large negative number the result is negative. If the small number is negative and the large number is positive, the result is positive.

The process which avoids the sign/magnitude problem is called *two's complement* arithmetic, as previously mentioned. Using two's complement arithmetic the numbers are signed as previously illustrated; that is, the most significant bit is zero for positive numbers, and one for negative numbers. The subtraction procedure using two's complement arithmetic permits the subtraction of positive and negative numbers without regard to sign or magnitude.

To find the two's complement of a number, all bits *including the sign bit*, are *complemented*; that is, all ones are changed to zero and all zeroes are changed to one. A binary one is then added to the number. The result is the two's complement. For example, a 4-bit binary representation of +7 is 0111. The two's complement is found by first complementing the number, giving 1000, then adding a binary 1. The result is 1001, which is the two's complement of 7.

Figure 3-5 shows the subtraction of +5 from +7, and +7 from +5. Note that when +7 is subtracted from +5 the answer is negative; therefore, the result is complemented to provide the correct answer.

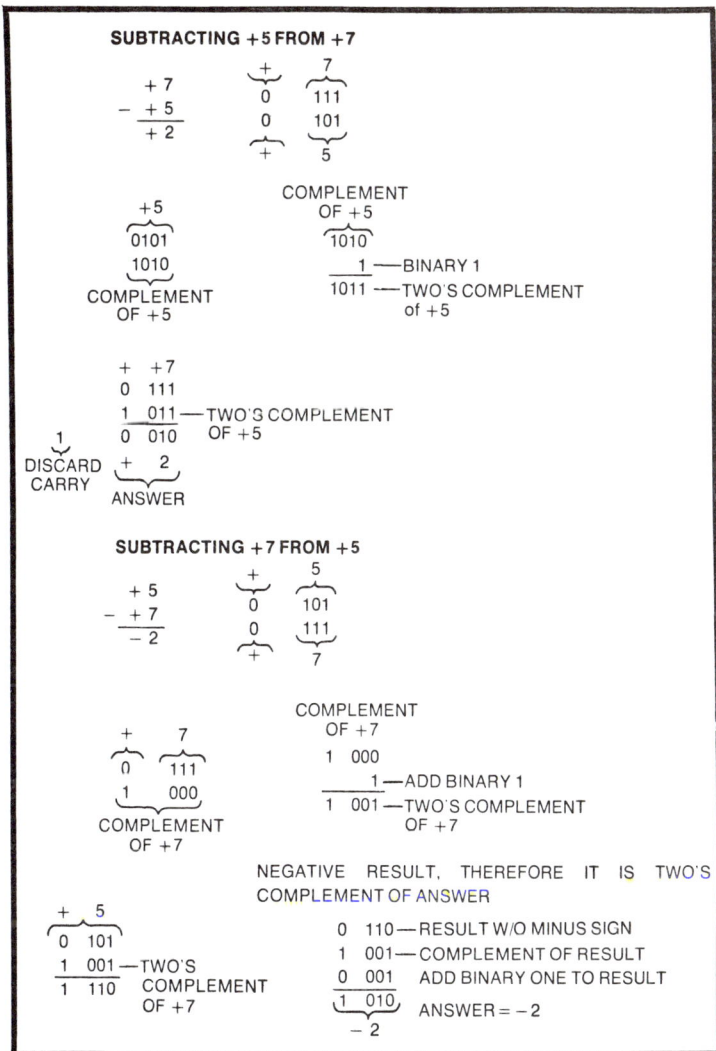

Fig. 3-5. Binary subtraction using two's complement arithmetic.

BINARY MULTIPLICATION AND DIVISION

Both multiplication and division are extensions of addition and subtraction. Multiplying 10 by 3 in decimal arithmetic simply says we add 10 to itself 3 times. Dividing 30 by 3 we simply say we subtract 3 from 30 until the result is zero, recording the number of subtractions. These same principles hold true for binary arithmetic. One of the major concepts in binary multiplication and division is that of shifting. Turning to the decimal for an example, we know that the number 100.02 is divided by 10 if the decimal point is shifted to the left one place. That is, 10.002 is 100.02 divided by 10. If the decimal point is shifted to the right, the number is multiplied. That is, 1000.2 is 100.02 multiplied by 10.

This same procedure may be used for binary multiplication. However, shifting the binary point to the right or to the left does not multiply the result by 10, but rather multiplies (or divides) the result by 2, the base of the number system in use. For example, 111.1 is the binary representation of the decimal number 7.5. Shifting the decimal point one place to the right results in the binary number 1111. The decimal is 15, or 2 × 7.5. On the other hand, if the binary point is shifted one place to the left, the binary number becomes 11.11. This represents the decimal number 3.75, (3 + 1/2 + 1/4).

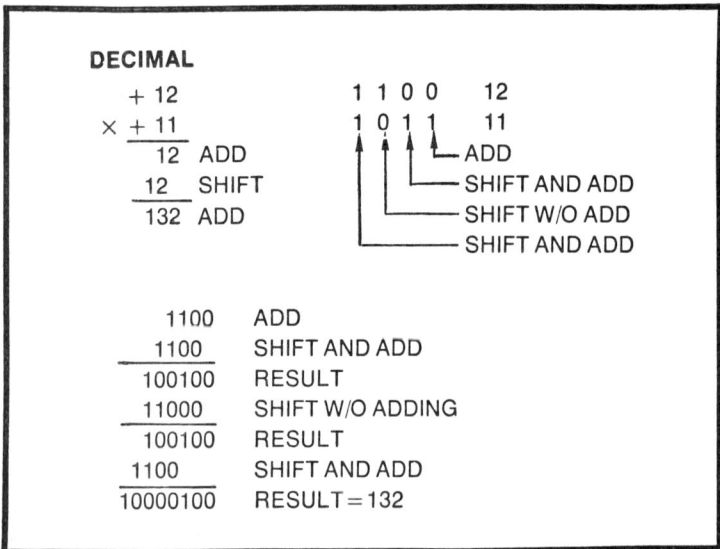

Fig. 3-6. Binary multiplication using the shift and add process. Note: Binary multiplication can involve signed numbers if two's complement arithmetic is used. Binary division is shift left and subtract using two's complement arithmetic.

In digital electronics, binary multiplication or division by 2s may be accomplished by the shifting process. A *shift left* is a division, and *shift right* is multiplication. Figure 3-6 illustrates a simple decimal multiplication problem followed by the equivalent binary process. If we look at this, we can see that really it is a *shift then add, shift then add,* process.

In the microprocessor, multiplication and division are done by the shifting and then adding or subtracting process. Usually the multiplication and division routines are programmed, not built into the microprocessor. Occasionally, the microprocessors have *hardware* multiply and divide capability. In such case, the shift and add or shift and subtract process is accomplished by the microprocessor, not by programming. This results in a much faster multiplication or division.

Chapter 4

Basic Logic

Microprocessors, like other forms of digital electronics, are based on the simple circuits of digital logic. Logic circuits are not new. As a matter of fact, digital circuits are really where the field of electronics began. Logic or digital circuits are as simple as a light switch. The light switch is fundamentally a digital circuit.

A digital circuit has two possible states. The light switch has these same two states: on and off. All digital circuitry is based around this simple concept. A circuit is either *on* or *off*. Analog electronics (the other half of the electronics world) is far more complicated, permitting signals to assume any level.

Having divided the electronics world into two camps, analog and digital, we may further break digital electronics into two types. *Combinational logic* refers to those digital circuits with a predictable output, given a set of input conditions. This predicted output changes if the given set of inputs are removed. *Sequential logic* refers to digital circuits which respond to certain input conditions and remembers those input conditions even after they are removed.

To summarize, there are two types of digital logic: combinational and sequential. Combinational circuits give us a predictable output for a set of inputs and sequential logic gives us memory.

COMBINATIONAL LOGIC

One of the finest characteristics of digital electronics is its simplicity. Combinational logic is no exception. In its basic form there are only two combinational logic circuits. These are called AND and OR. We can think of both AND gates and

OR gates as black boxes with unique responses (outputs) to ON and OFF input combinations. Frequently we do not speak of ONs and OFFs but logic "1s" and logic "0s", or TRUE and FALSE. Often one and zero are simply reduced to "1" and "0".

Most commonly the relationship between logic 1s and 0s and electrical signals is 1 is a high and 0 is a low. This may be translated to 1 is a closed switch, the value of voltage used for supply (B+ or V_{cc}) or simply the most positive voltage in the circuit. In these situations logic 0 takes on the opposite definition. That is, a logic 0 may be: an open switch, ground (the return voltage level), or the most negative voltage in the circuit. These two sets of electrical definitions for logic 1 and logic 0 are commonly called *positive true logic*. Reviewing these definitions we can easily see how the term positive true logic comes about. The true condition is then represented by the most positive signal in the circuit. Remember, digital circuits, by definition, only have a most positive or most negative (least positive) condition. There are no in-between conditions.

If there is a positive true logic there must be a negative true logic. *Negative true logic* assumes a logic 1 (a true) is the most negative signal in the circuit. Likewise, negative true logic assumes a logic 0 to be the most positive signal in the circuit. Obviously how you define the signals in a circuit (positive true or negative true) does make a difference in the circuit operation. The exact differences are treated in a later section. For now, assume all circuits are defined as positive true logic.

THE AND GATE

As noted earlier, the AND gate is a fundamental building block in combinational logic. The simple circuit of Fig. 4-1 performs the AND function. The term AND is derived from the condition required to turn the lamp on. The lamp is *on* when switches A *and* B are closed. A third switch is added to the diagram in Fig. 4-1B. The lamp in Fig. 4-1B turns *on* when switches A *and* B *and* C are closed. Note: In these particular examples, the closed position of the switch and the *on* condition of the lamp are defined as a logic one. When the switches are open, or the lamp is *off*, they are defined as zeros.

The logical concept of AND is not limited to electronic circuits. For example, to start your car, you must have gas in the tank *and* a key in the ignition.

Switches and lamps are not the common parts used in logic circuits, although they do perform the logical functions

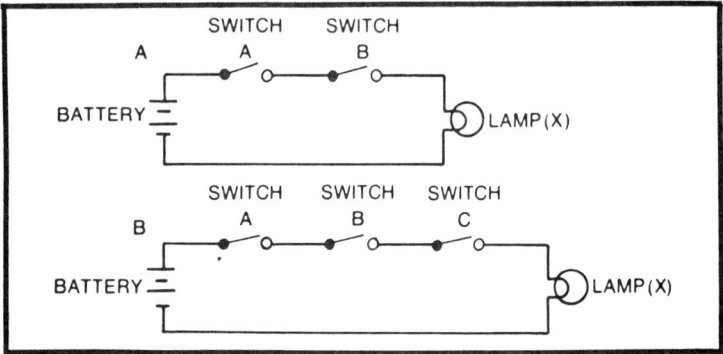

Fig. 4-1. The circuit at A represents a 2-switch AND gate. The lamp is on when switch A AND B are closed. At B, the three switches represent a 3-input AND gate. Like the gate at A, the lamp is on when all switches are closed, A **and** B and C. Note that it is also correct to say the lamp is off if switch A or B or C is open.

and properly demonstrate logical actions. Today there are *integrated circuits* (ICs) which serve as *black boxes* to perform these functions. These digital ICs come in many functions and a number of the simpler functions may come in one IC package. For example, four AND gates may be found in one IC.

Continuous redrawing of the transistors, diodes, and resistors in these ICs is meaningless and unduly complicates matters. For this reason a symbol is used indicating the logical function performed by this IC building block. Figure 4-2 shows the symbol for the AND function. There may be as many inputs as desired even though this Figure only shows three. Letters such as A, B, C, etc., are used to identify the various gate inputs. Letters at the end of the alphabet are used to indicate the output. In Fig. 4-2 the letter "X" is used to indicate the output. An equation is also shown in Fig. 4-2. This equation, written in *Boolean algebra*, states the output X is true (1) when

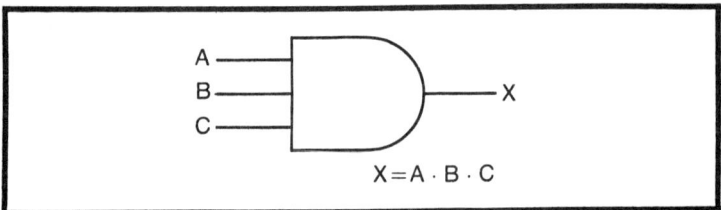

Fig. 4-2. The standard symbol for an AND gate. This particular symbol shows three inputs and is the symbol which represents the circuit of Fig. 4-1B. The input lines are the switches and the lamp is the output. Also shown in this figure is the Boolean equation for a 3-input AND gate.

the inputs A *and* B, *and*, C, are true (1s). The dots between the letters are read as AND, not times. Occasionally a cross (×) is used to indicate the AND function. Again, this must not be confused with the concept of multiplication from ordinary algebra.

Figure 4-3 shows the *truth tables* for the AND gate. Truth tables are frequently easier to understand than Boolean expressions for the particular gate. The truth table gives the gate output for *all* possible input combinations. Figure 4-3A gives the *electrical* truth table for a two input AND gate. Looking at this truth table we can see the output is HIGH only when input A *and* B are HIGH. In Fig. 4-3B we have converted the HIGH/LOW electrical signals into logic 1s and 0s. This truth table indicates the output is 1 only for a logic 1 at input A *and* a logic 1 at input B.

Truth tables, like the gates they represent, are not confined to only two inputs. Figure 4-4 shows the logical truth table for a four-input AND gate. The appropriate symbol and the Boolean equation are also shown. As can be seen, the size of the truth table becomes larger as the number of inputs increases. An 8-input gate requires 256 lines to represent all possible combinations of input signals. When they become this large, it is better to remember the function of the gate by its name rather than by a truth table.

THE OR GATE

The second fundamental building block of digital electronics is the *OR* gate. Like the *AND* gate, one can guess the function from the name. Figure 4-5 gives us the simple switch equivalent of a three-input OR gate. From this simple diagram one can see the lamp is *on* if switch A *or* B, *or* C is closed.

Once again, the actual number of inputs to the OR gate is only limited by the need for OR signals. OR gates may come

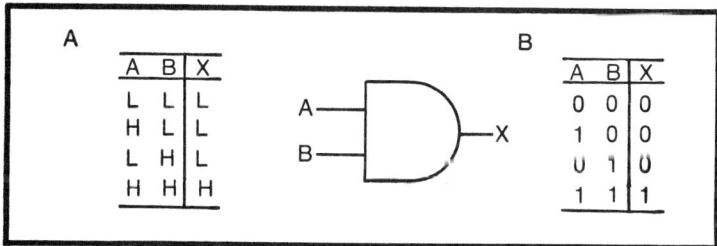

A				B		
A	B	X		A	B	X
L	L	L		0	0	0
H	L	L		1	0	0
L	H	L		0	1	0
H	H	H		1	1	1

Fig. 4-3. The truth table at A shows electrical designations for a two-input AND gate. The truth table at B shows logic designations for the same gate. Note that the only difference between the two tables is that the electrical highs and lows have been changed to logic 1s and 0s, respectively.

45

A	B	C	D	X
0	0	0	0	0
0	0	0	1	0
0	0	1	0	0
0	0	1	1	0
0	1	0	0	0
0	1	0	1	0
0	1	1	0	0
0	1	1	1	0
1	0	0	0	0
1	0	0	1	0
1	0	1	0	0
1	0	1	1	0
1	1	0	0	0
1	1	0	1	0
1	1	1	0	0
1	1	1	1	1

$$X = A \cdot B \cdot C \cdot D$$

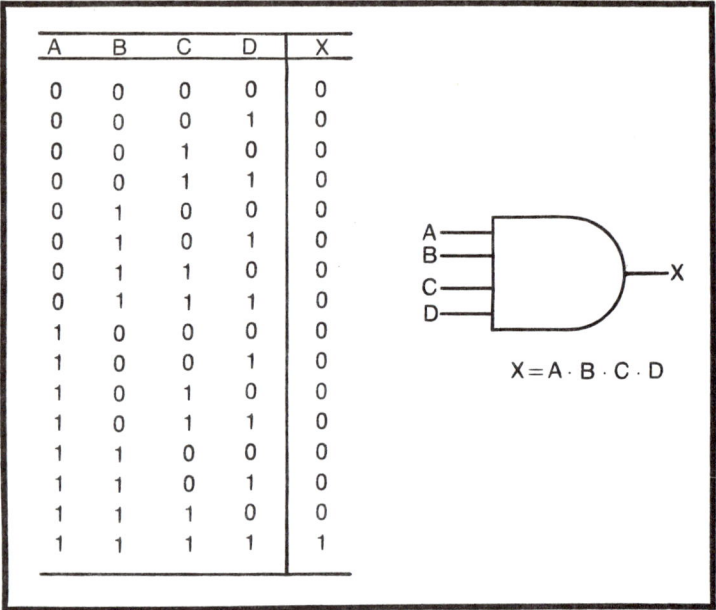

Fig. 4-4. The truth table and the logic symbol for a 4-input AND gate. Note there are 16 different possible combinations of 1s and 0s for a 4-input gate. ($2^4 = 16$).

with as few as two inputs and some have eight or more inputs. The OR function, like the AND function, is not exclusively found in digital electronics. For example, your car starts if you use the key or if a burlgar hot wires the ignition!

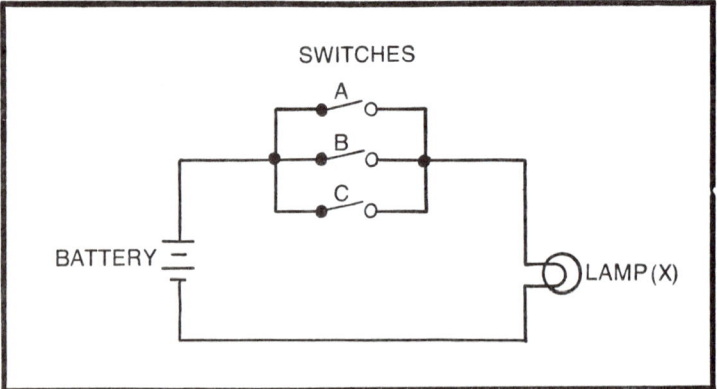

Fig. 4-5. A 4-switch OR gate. The lamp is on when Switch A OR B OR C is closed.

Figure 4-6 gives the logical symbol used for the OR function. The Boolean equation and the truth table for a three-input OR gate are also given. Note the Boolean equation uses the "+" symbol for the OR operator. This must not be confused with the *plus* operator of ordinary algebra.

Looking at the truth table we can easily see the output is a logic 1 if there is a logic 1 on inputs A *or* B *or* C. Also note that the output is a logic 1 when there is a combination of logic 1s and 0s on the gate input and when all the inputs are 1s.

THE INVERTER

We have now defined two of the basic logical functions. These are mixed and combined to provide a vast array of functions used to create a complex device like a microprocessor.

These two functions, AND and OR, may be modified by the process of inversion. The inverter is a simple device which may be applied to any logic signal. The inverter simply takes a logic 1 and makes it a logic 0. Likewise a logic 0 is made into a logic 1.

Like the AND gate and the OR gate, the inverter has a standard symbol, a Boolean equation, and a truth table. The inverter symbol, Boolean equation, and truth table, are shown in Fig. 4-7. Althouth this is the most common representation of the inverter, one should note that the inversion is indicated by the small circle at the output of the inverter, *not* by the triangle. This point becomes more clear as we progress into circuits which use the inverter in combination with other logic elements.

The Boolean equation brings the *NOT bar* to light. The equation shows the output of the inverter is $\bar{A}$. This is read as

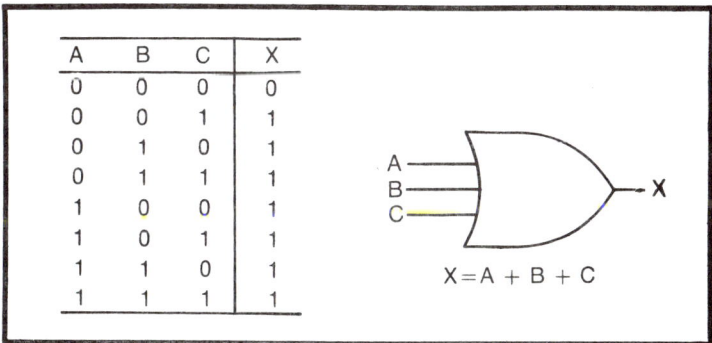

A	B	C	X
0	0	0	0
0	0	1	1
0	1	0	1
0	1	1	1
1	0	0	1
1	0	1	1
1	1	0	1
1	1	1	1

$$X = A + B + C$$

Fig. 4-6. The logic symbol, the Boolean equation, and the logical truth table for the 3-input OR gate

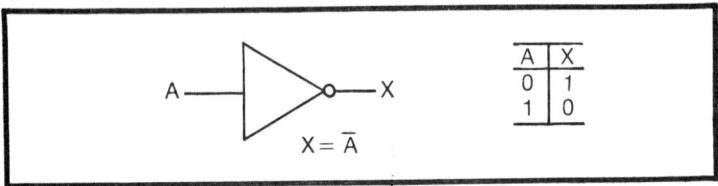

Fig. 4-7. The logic symbol, the Boolean equation, and the truth table for the inverter. The inverter accomplishes the NOT, or complementing function.

"NOT A", or as "A bar". The line over the top of A indicates the signal at that point in the circuit is logically the opposite of the signal at point A. This entire concept is easily expressed by the truth table shown in Fig. 4-7.

With the AND, OR and INVERT (NOT) functions in hand we are now able to build virtually any digital circuit we wish.

THE NAND GATE

The NAND gate is one of the first simple combinations of gates and inverters. Figure 4-8 shows the AND gate driving an INVERTER. Also shown are the Boolean equations for each circuit point. Note that the AND gate output is as we expected. The output of the inverter is an inversion of the *entire* AND expression. Figure 4-8 also gives a combination truth table.

The combined symbol for the NAND gate, the Boolean equation for the NAND gate and the truth table for the NAND gate are given in Fig. 4-9. Again keep in mind the NAND gate is not limited to two inputs. Inputs may be added as needed to the NAND gate just as to the AND and OR gates.

THE NOR GATE

If there is a NAND gate, then there must be a NOR gate. Figure 4-10 shows the logical development of the NOR gate

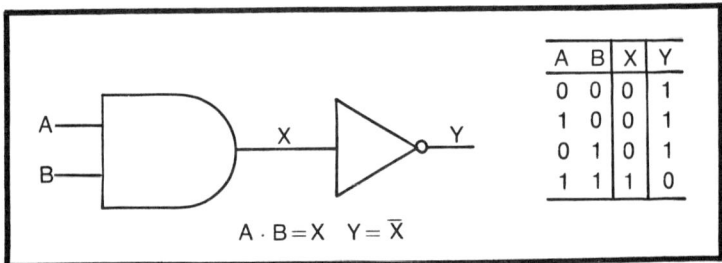

Fig. 4-8. Building the NAND gate using the AND gate and the INVERTER. The truth table shows the output from the AND gate as X and the output of the inverter (the inverted output of the AND gate) as Y.

48

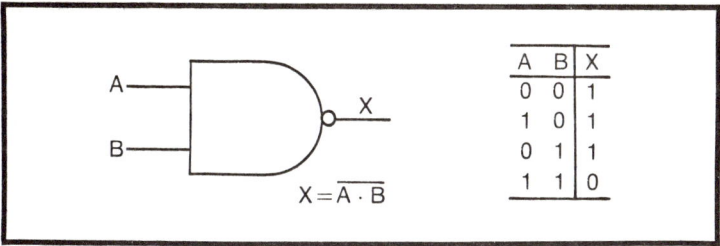

Fig. 4-9. The logic symbol, the Boolean equation, and the truth table for the NAND gate. Note that the small circle at the output of the NAND gate indicates the output is inverted. This circle changes the gate from AND to NAND.

from an OR gate and an INVERTER. The output of the NOR gate is $Y = \overline{A + B}$, not $Y = \overline{A} + \overline{B}$, which is an entirely different condition than NOR.

NAND and NOR gates are the most popular forms of integrated circuit logic. There are two reasons for this. First, they are simpler to build than either AND or OR. Second, they are far more versatile when used to implement logical circuits.

One example of this versatility is shown in Fig. 4-11. Both the NAND gate and the NOR gate are used to create inverters. This saves part for the logic designer. Both NAND (or NOR) gates and INVERTERS are not needed.

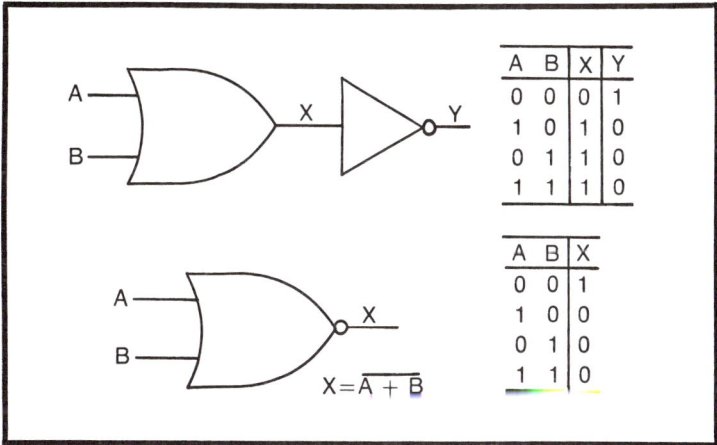

Fig. 4-10. Developing the NOR gate from the OR gate and an INVERTER. Also shown are the truth tables for the development of the gate and for the NOR gate. The symbol for the NOR gate and the Boolean equation for the NOR gate are also shown. Note the small circle on the output of the NOR gate. This small circle changes the symbol from an OR gate to a NOR gate.

49

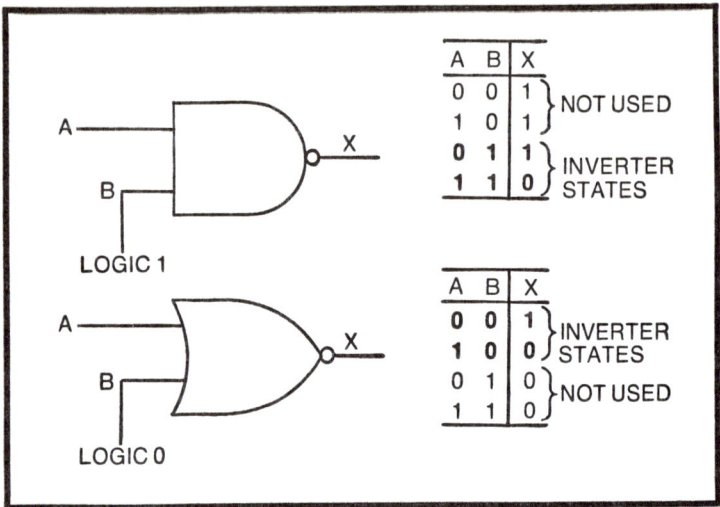

Fig. 4-11. Using the NAND gate and the NOR gate as an INVERTER. To use the NAND gate as an inverter the unused input must be "tied high" (connected to a logic 1). To use the NOR gate as an inverter the unused input must be "tied low" (connected to a logic 0).

Because the NAND and the NOR gates contain the INVERT function, any of the basic gates may be created. This is shown in Fig. 4-12. The proof of these gate combinations is beyond the scope of this book. However, the reader can find the proof in more advanced logic texts or can prove the equalities by use of truth tables.

As noted earlier, we have presumed positive true logic for all examples. Negative true logic changes the logic function of a particular *electrical* implementation of a gate. This can easily be demonstrated by using our example of the car. The original example used the AND function. To start your car you must have gas in the tank *and* a key in the ignition. Applying negative logic to the same hardware (the car, gas, and key) we change the function from AND to OR. This is to say, your car does not start if you *do not* have gas in the tank, *or* you *do not* have a key in the ignition.

In a similar manner we may invert our definitions regarding the electrical equivalence of the logic signals into a gate. This changes its logical function. Note: in both cases the hardware (and therefore the electrical response) remains the same. The logical response of circuit changes with the change in logic levels definition. Frequently microprocessor engineers change from positive true logic to negative true logic to obtain the optimum electrical performance from the ICs at hand.

APPLYING THE GATES TO MICROPROCESSOR CIRCUITS

Now that we have developed the basic gate functions for combinational logic, we can develop a few examples. These examples are ones found frequently in the microprocessor iteslf or as logic circuits supporting the microprocessor. Although only three examples of combinational logic circuits are presented here, a great many others exist and are commonly used with microprocessors.

THE DECODER

The *decoder* is a common function in many microprocessor circuits. It uses combinational logic. Decoders are used to select one object of many. The selecting or input number is in binary form.

One of the most common uses of the decoder is the addressing of memory words. For example, a simple microprocessor system may have 4096 words of memory (4K). Obviously, 4096 separate lines cannot connect the microprocessor to the memory. The memory is connected to the processor by 12 lines. All the possible combinations of 1s and 0s that can appear on 12 lines total 4096 ($2^{12} = 4096$). Inside the memory, we still must address cach of the 4096 words separately. Here the decoder comes into play. A 12-line-to-4096-line decoder is employed to perform this selection.

Figure 4-13 shows a simplified form of decoding action. In this example, four memory cells are addressed. Each cell is addressed when a logic 1 is applied. Although there are four memory cells, they are addressed by only two lines. These lines have four possible combinations:

00
10
01, and
11

The function of the decoder is to convert the two lines of binary information into selecting information for the four memory cells. The table gives the desired selecting sequence for the memory cells. The decoder selects cell number one when the AB signal is a 00. A 00 at the inverter inputs gives a 1 at the outputs. The inputs to AND gate number one are connected to the inverter outputs. Therefore, a 00 output at the AB input results in a 11 input to gate number 1. Memory cell one is therefore selected. Looking at the diagram in Fig. 4-13 we can see that no other gate has a 11 combination at its input.

NOR GATES

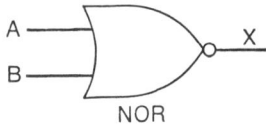

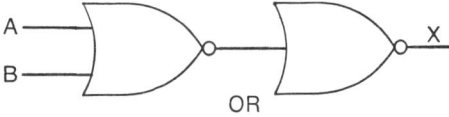

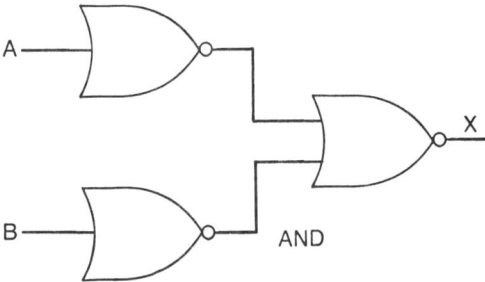

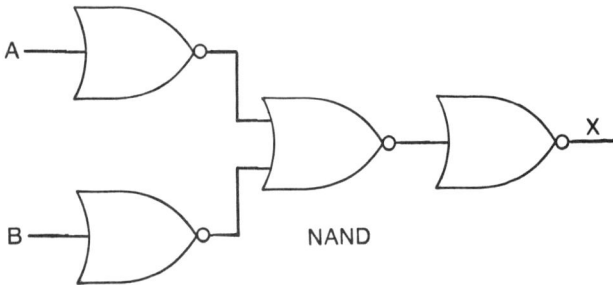

According to the rules for the AND gate, no other gate output is at a logic 1.

If, for example, the 01 combination were to be applied to decoder input AB, memory cell 3 is selected by the following process. The inverted signal from A is applied to an input of gate three. This is a logic one. The other input to gate three is connected directly to input B. It therefore also receives a logic 1. With a logic 1 at both inputs, the output of gate three is a logic one. Memory cell three is selected. No other gate

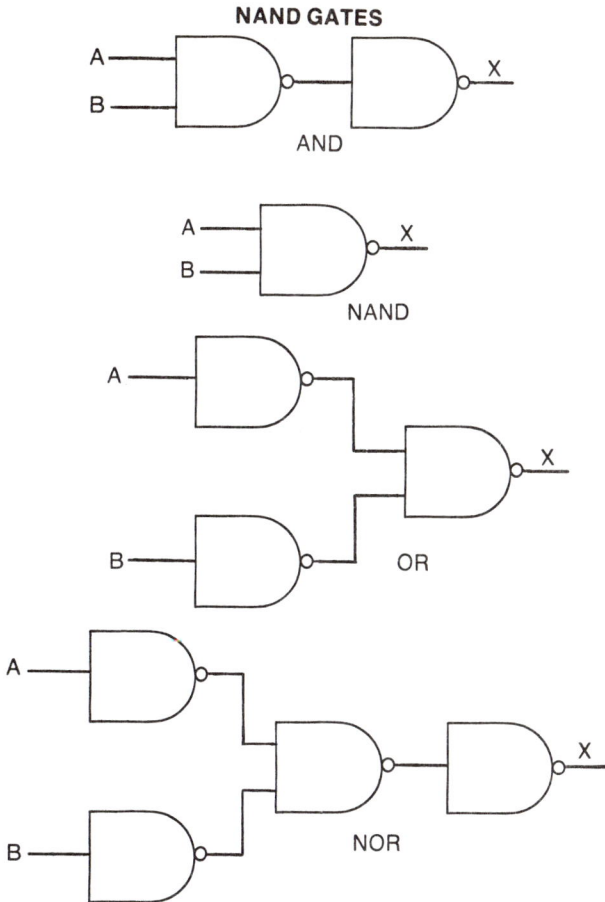

NAND GATES

AND

NAND

OR

NOR

Fig. 4-12. Building any of the gates from either the NAND or the NOR. Note: Unused NAND gate inputs must be "tied high" and unused NOR gate inputs must be "tied low." This table demonstrates the versatility of the inverted gate types as compared to the noninverted gate types.

receives a 11 combination at its input. Therefore, memory cell three is the only one selected by a 01 input at AB.

The simple decoder of Fig 4-13 can be easily expanded. With one more input line, one more inverter, and eight three-input AND gates, the decoder converts three lines into a selection of one of eight.

If the memory cells require a logic 0 for selection rather than a logic 1, NAND gates can be used. The NAND gates provide the AND function as well as providing the INVERT function required for the memory select.

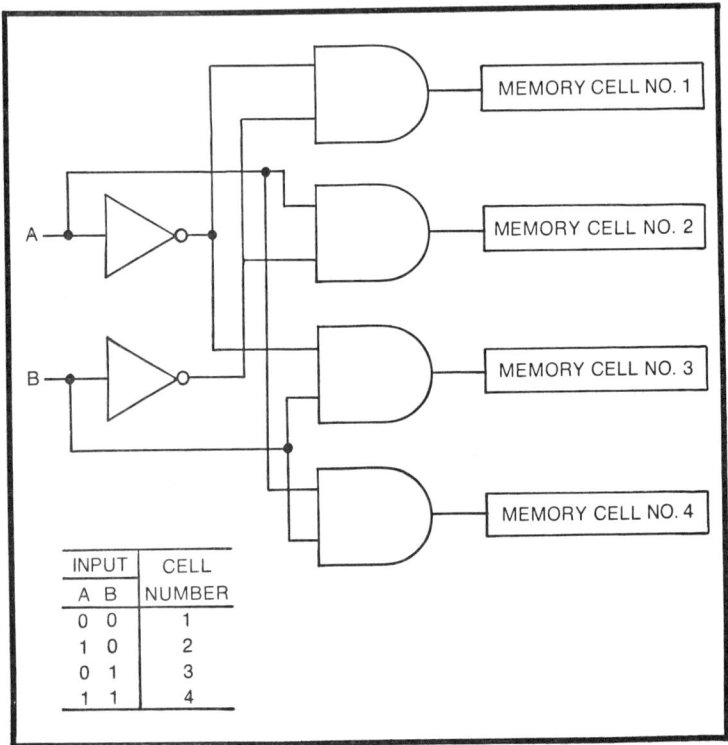

Fig. 4-13. A 2-line-to-4-line decoder. The information on the two lines is in binary format. The information on the 4-line output is in 1-of-4 format.

THE MULTIPLEXER

Another common function required in microprocessors is *multiplexing*. Multiplexing is connecting one of a number of signals to a single output. Multiplexers are like gates. They have many inputs and only one output.

A multiplexer, for example, could connect the output of register A, B, C, or the data bus to the Arithmetic and Logic Unit (ALU) input. Figure 4-14 shows a multiplexer as a simple rotary switch. A multiplexer which does the same job but with AND gates is also shown.

In this example, a logic 1 is applied to the AND gate that is to pass the signal to the OR gate. The gates act as their names imply. They either pass or block the digital signal flow. The OR gate at the output of the multiplexer combines the AND gates outputs into one line.

To avoid using four separate lines to control the multiplexer input selection, a decoder can drive the control lines. The multiplexer input selection is then done, not by a logic 1 on one of four lines, but by proper combinations of ones and zeros on two lines. This in fact, is the most common form of the multiplexer.

THE EXCLUSIVE OR/NOR

The EXCLUSIVE OR gate and its inverted counterpart the EXCLUSIVE NOR are special versions of the OR and NOR gates. They may be created by use of NAND or NOR gates. The EXCLUSIVE OR gate has special significance to those interested in microprocessors. It is the basic logical element used to perform binary arithmetic.

Figure 4-15 shows the symbol, the Boolean equations and the truth table for the EXCLUSIVE OR gate. For reference the truth table for the OR gate is shown in the boxed area. Note the major difference between the OR gate and the EXCLUSIVE OR gate. The OR gate (sometimes called the INCLUSIVE OR) includes the AND function. The EXCLUSIVE OR does not.

Figure 4-16 shows the inverted counterpart to the EXCLUSIVE OR, the EXCLUSIVE NOR. The truth table

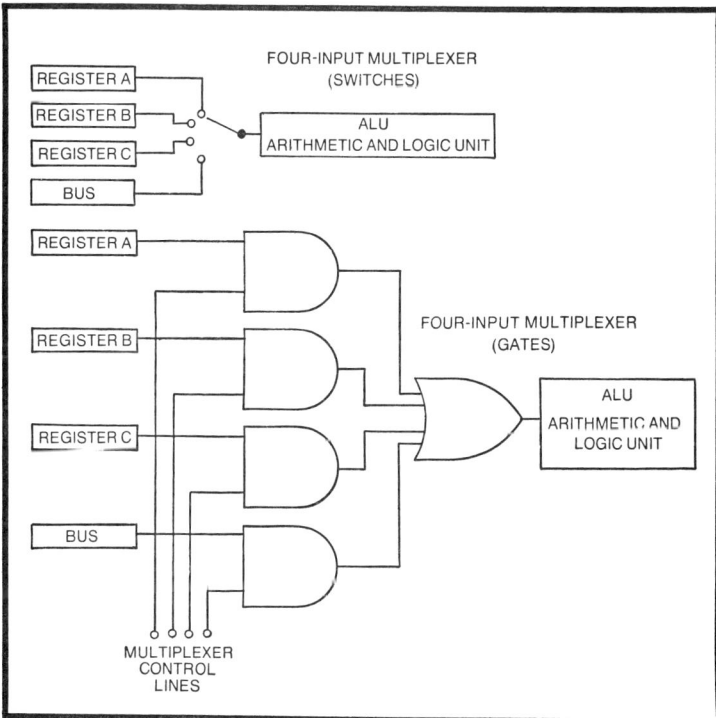

Fig. 4-14. A 4-input multiplexer. Both the switch implementation of this multiplexer and the gate implementation of this multiplexer are shown.

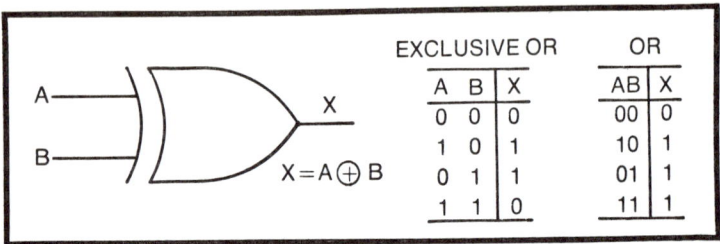

Fig. 4-15. The 2-input EXCLUSIVE OR gate. Note the double back on the EXCLUSIVE OR input side of the symbol.

shows one of the uses for the EXCLUSIVE NOR. If both gate inputs are identical (both 1s or both 0s), the output is a one. If they are not equal, the output is a zero. This circuit can be easily expanded to compare many lines of digital information for equality.

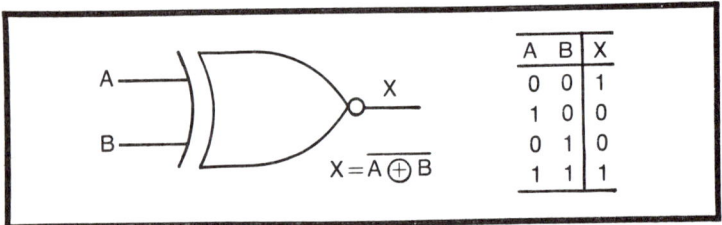

Fig. 4-16. The EXCLUSIVE NOR gate. Note the truth table shows a logic 1 at the output for identical inputs.

Figure 4-17 shows the EXCLUSIVE OR built with NAND gates. The EXCLUSIVE OR can also be built with NOR gates. To do this requires five two-input NOR gates. Commonly four two-input gates come on one IC.

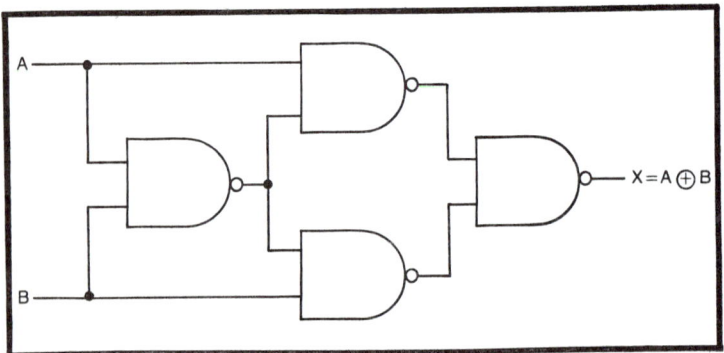

Fig. 4-17. The EXCLUSIVE OR built with NAND gates. Note that this is the number of 2-input NAND gates normally found in an IC package.

Figure 4-18 shows the EXCLUSIVE OR used in a *full adder*. The input to the full adder is two binary digits (bits), A and B. It adds them according to the rules of binary arithmetic and produces the sum at the output (Σ). A carry is also generated if required. The full adder has provision to include the carry from any previous additions. The full adder is used in microprocessors to accomplish all its arithmetic functions. Subtraction, multiplication, and division are simply modifications upon the process of addition.

A series of full adders is shown in Fig. 4-19. Four full adders are used to add two four-bit numbers. ($A_0 - A_3$ add $B_0 - B_3$). The result is a four bit number ($\Sigma_0 - \Sigma_3$) and any carry (C).

SEQUENTIAL LOGIC

Combinational logic permits the combination of various logic signals with a predictable output. The concept of time is not yet introduced. Often we wish to store the results of digital processing. We then come back, at some unspecified time, and retrieve those results. The introduction of time to logic circuits requires *sequential logic*.

One of the most common examples of the need for sequential logic is the microprocessor memory. The answer to a particular computation is stored so we may come back at some later time and refer to it. Sequential logic helps with microprocessor arithmetic functions and is used with some of the communications functions.

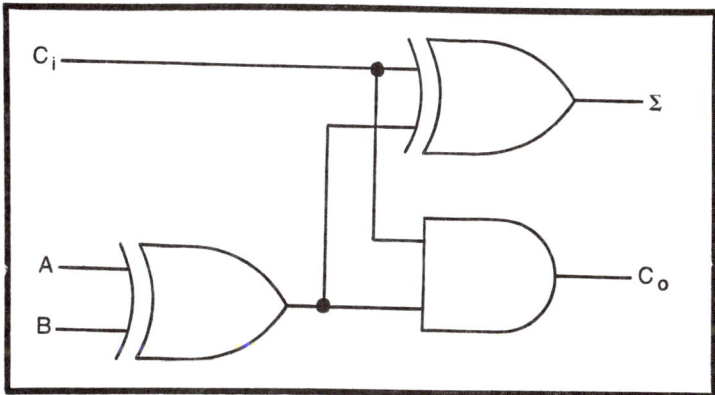

Fig. 4-18. Using two EXCLUSIVE OR gates and one AND gate to build a full adder. Note that the full adder has three inputs. A and B are the lines to be added and C is the carry from any previous additions. The output is the sum of A and B, and the C output is any carry generated in the addition process.

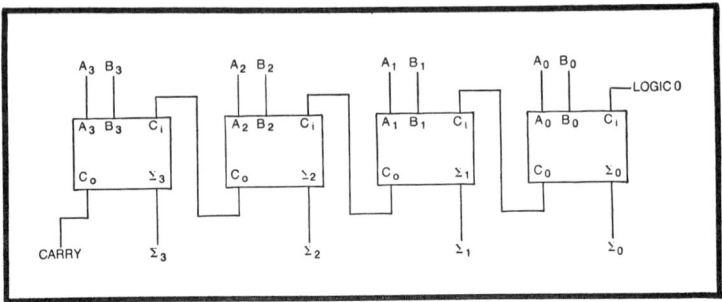

Fig. 4-19. Using four full adders to perform a parallel addition of two 4-bit binary numbers. Note the carry from the first adder is connected to the carry input of the second adder.

THE LATCH

The simplest form of digital storage is the *latch*. A simple latch is shown in Fig. 4-20. The latch is made of two cross-coupled NAND gates. A latch must meet two requirements. First, it must permanently retain its output state. Second, it must have two inputs permitting its output to be set (logic 1) or reset (logic 0).

The following explains operation of the latch of Fig. 4-20:

1. assume both inputs at logic one;
2. assume output Q at logic 1;
3. the gate-2 inputs are 11;
4. the result of a 11 input to a NAND gate is a logic 0;
5. the gate-1 inputs are 10;

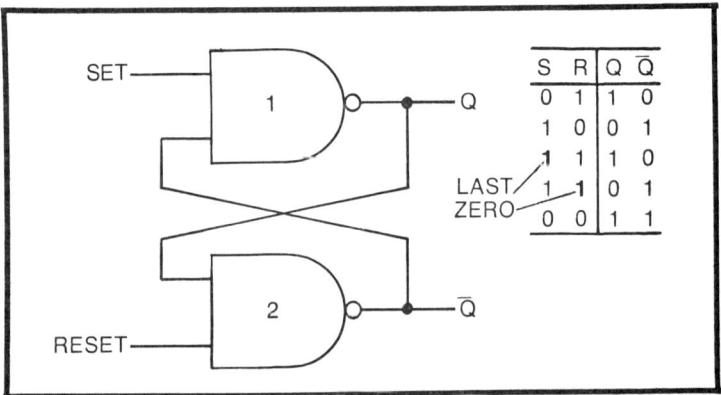

Fig. 4-20. Cross-coupled gates, or the simple latch. As shown by the truth table, the output can tell an observer where the last zero occurred, on the set or on the reset input.

58

6. the result of a 10 input to a NAND gate is a logic 1;

7. these conditions give stable condition at the latch Q and $\bar{Q}$ outputs.

If we now wish to change the latch output, a momentary logic 0 is applied to the reset input. This momentary zero at the reset input triggers the following sequence:

1. the 11 at the gate-2 input is changed to a 10;

2. the gate-2 output changes from a logic 0 to a logic 1;

3. the 1 at $\bar{Q}$ produces a 11 at the gate-1 input;

4. an 11 at gate-1 produces a 0 at Q;

5. the zero at Q ensures a 1 at $\bar{Q}$;

6. the latch Q and $\bar{Q}$ outputs are changed from 1 0 to 0 1;

7. the output state remains unchanged until a logic 0 is applied to the set input.

This basic latch suffers from some problems. The two outputs Q and $\bar{Q}$ should be complementary (i.e., one a zero and the other a one). This is not always the case. When zeros are applied to both the set and reset inputs both outputs become logic 1s. Fortunately, this problem can be fixed by the addition of some extra gates.

The basic latch remains in either the set or the reset state as long as power is applied. Examining the latch outputs when both inputs are logic one, the outputs tell what happened last. Looking at the truth table in Fig. 4-20 we can see a 1 at Q indicates the last zero was at the set input. This simple circuit is the basis of all memories.

Gated Latch

The extra gates are shown in Fig. 4-21. This circuit is called the *gated latch*. The two latch-input gates permit

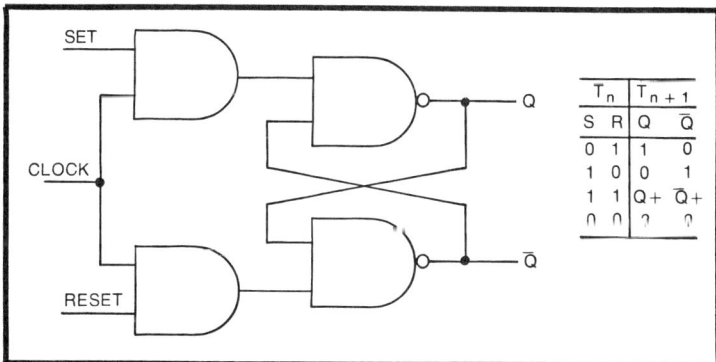

Fig. 4-21. The gated latch. The 2-input AND gates allow the user to control the time when signals reach the set and reset inputs of the latch.

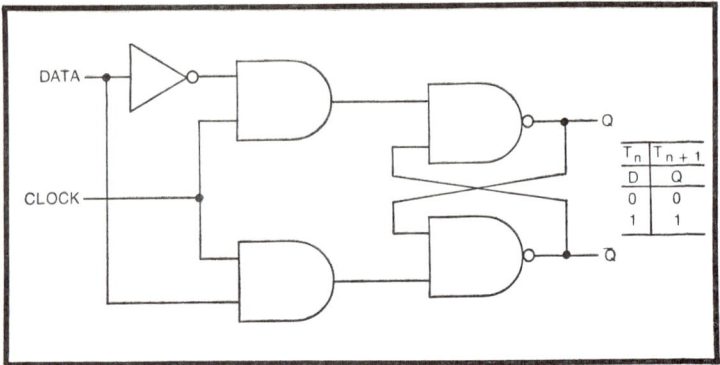

Fig. 4-22. The data latch. A common form of the gated latch where the user does not have to supply both set and reset information. Four or eight data latches are often found in one IC package.

control of the time when the latch responds to set and reset signals. When the clock line is logic 1, the set and reset lines can change the latch output. When the clock line is logic 0 the set and reset lines are disconnected from the latch. This condition is shown in the truth table in Fig. 4-21. The truth table now shows the logic values of set and reset at time T, before the clock pulse. It also shows the value of Q at time $T + 1$ (after the clock pulse). If a 11 signal is applied to the set/reset inputs there is no change in the latch output state. This is indicated by the Q_t in the truth table. Q_t indicates Q is the same at $T + 1$ as it was at time T. When set and reset are 01 or 10, the output follows according to the truth table. If both the inputs are zero, the status of Q after the clock pulse is unknown. It is unknown because the last zero on the *latch* input depends on the electrical parameters of the two gates used, not on any logical set of circumstances.

Gated latches are extremely common in microprocessor circuits. Often there are two or four gated latches in one IC, all utilizing a common clock line. Such devices are referred to as *dual* or *quad latches*.

Data Latch

A special verson of the gated latch supplies reset information to the set input via an inverter. This configuration allows the user to supply information to the latch as single-line digital information. This form of latch shown in Fig. 4-22 is called the *data latch*. The gated latch is not completely free of problems. For those conditions where the gated latch causes problems, the J-K flip-flop is used.

60

THE J-K AND D-TYPE FLIP FLOPS

The major problem with the gated latch occurs during the clock pulse. At the time the clock is high the latch output is no longer protected. What is needed at this time is a latch which effectively works on the edge of the clock pulse. The *J-K flip-flop* consists of two gated latches in series. Data is admitted to the first latch, or *master* gated latch, when the clock pulse goes high. Data is transferred from the first latch to the second latch (the *slave*) when the clock pulse goes low. The internal workings of the J-K flip-flop are complex. There is no need to look at it from the gate level. Therefore, Fig. 4-23 shows the block representation of the J-K flip-flop and the associated truth table.

Figure 4-23 brings out some unique features of the J-K flip-flop. First, the truth table shows the same conditions as the gated latch with the exception of the 11 input condition. The two inputs formerly called set and reset are now renamed J and K. When they are in the 11 state the truth table tells us the output is $\bar{Q}_t$ after the clock pulse. This means it is the logical opposite condition found at Q prior to the clock pulse.

The lower part of Fig. 4-23 shows two waveforms. On the vertical axis, we show a logic 0 as a low line and a logic 1 as a

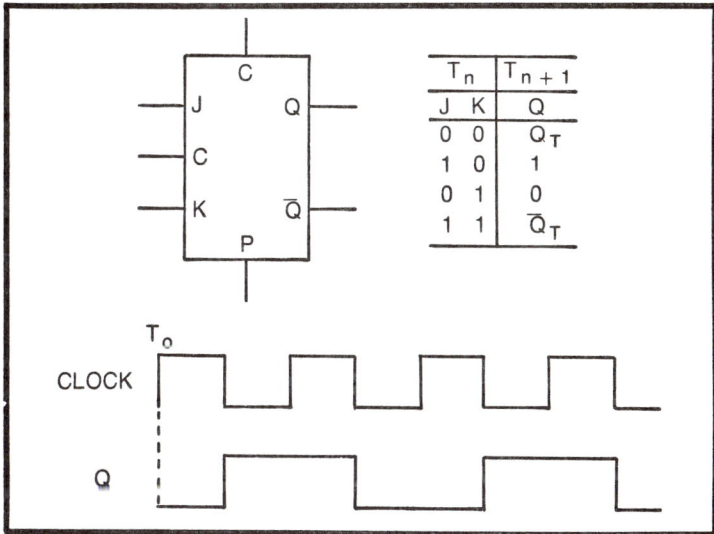

T_n		T_{n+1}
J	K	Q
0	0	Q_T
1	0	1
0	1	0
1	1	$\bar{Q}_T$

Fig. 4-23. The J-K flip-flop. The symbol for the flip-flop shows the J and K inputs, the Clock input, and the preset and Clear inputs. Q and $\bar{Q}$ are the outputs. The J-K flip-flop truth table shows that all four input conditions provide useful output conditions, unlike all previous flip-flops. The waveforms show the J-K flip-flop being used as a divide-by-2 circuit.

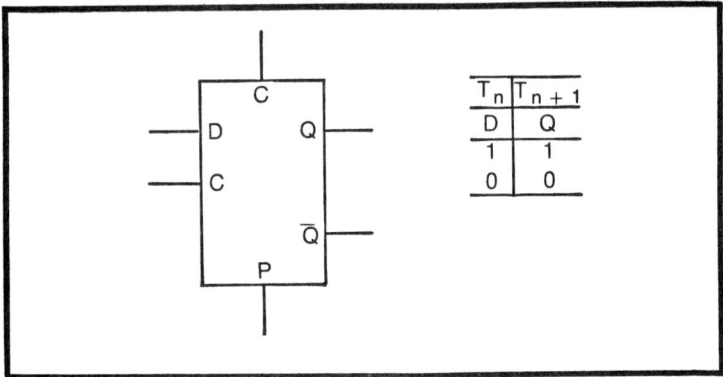

Fig. 4-24. The D-Type edge triggered flip-flop. Note that the truth table is identical to the data latch truth table. The difference between this flip-flop and the data latch lies in the edge triggering of the information into the outputs rather than clocking the information through on a clock high.

high line. The horizontal line is time. Starting at the left edge is a point called T_0. T_0 is the time we started observing the flip-flop. As time passes, the clock signal becomes a one and then a zero. It keeps repeating this cycle. The number of complete cycles which occur in one second is the frequency of the signal. Frequency is expressed in hertz (Hz).

The two waveforms show what happens at Q compared to the clock signal. Each time the clock pulse goes from one to zero, Q changes state. Another way of stating this is to note the waveform at Q is *one-half* the frequency of the waveform at the clock input. Dividing a frequency by two is one of the classic uses of the flip-flop. However, as we have seen from previous discussion, this is only a small fraction of the flip-flop's capabilities.

Figure 4-23 also shows two additional flip-flop inputs. These are labeled C for *clear* and P for *preset*. A logic zero applied to the clear input *at any time* results in Q going to a 0. A logic 0 applied to the preset input of the flip-flop results in a logic 1 at Q. Both of these functions override any action at the J, K, or clock inputs. Presetting and clearing are important as they allow initialization of the flip-flop outputs.

It should be noted some forms of J-K flip-flops may be found with various multiple input gates at the J and K inputs. When this is the case the J and K signals are true when the output of the indicated gate is true.

A special version of the J-K flip-flop is called the *D-type edge triggered flip-flop*. The D-type flip-flop is used in many microprocessor control and status applications. The truth and logic symbol for the D-type edge triggered flip-flop are given in Fig. 4-24. The major difference between these two flip-flops, other than shown by the truth tables, lies in the clock signals. The J-K flip-flop changes output state on the *trailing edge* (one-to-zero change) of the clock waveform. The D-type edge triggered flip-flop changes output state on the *leading edge* (zero-to-one change) of the D clock waveform. The D-type flip-flop may be made to *toggle* (divide-by-2) like the J-K flip-flop if the $\overline{Q}$ output is connected to the D input.

Figure 4-25 shows a D-type edge triggered flip-flop used to toggle. The associated clock and Q waveforms are also shown. Note the waveform shows the difference between the leading-edge trigger and the trailing-edge trigger.

THE REGISTER

Registers are a fundamental microprocessor component. Microprocessors do not work with digital signals a single bit at a time. This is an important concept which you should thoroughly understand so you later can understand many of the microprocessor internal workings. The microprocessor process digital words in *parallel* rather than in *series*. To understand the difference between parallel and serial processing, consider your approach to the following addition:

$$
\begin{array}{r}
12567 \\
35378 \\
\hline
47945
\end{array}
$$

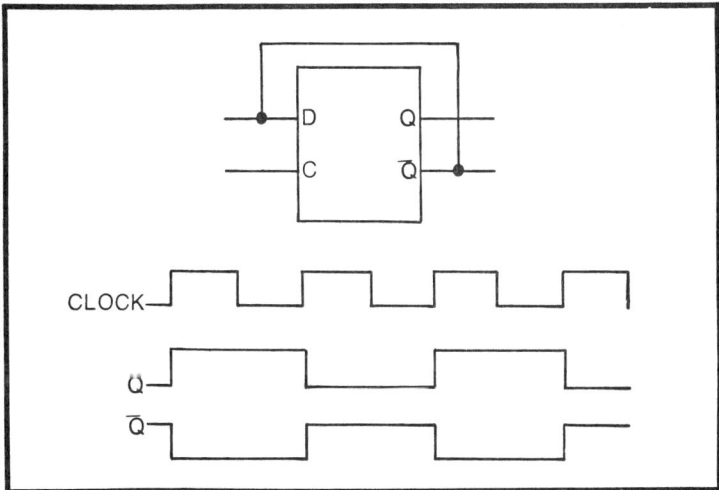

Fig. 4-25. Using the D-Type edge triggered flip-flop in a divide-by-2 mode. Note the Q output is wired back to the D input to accomplish this.

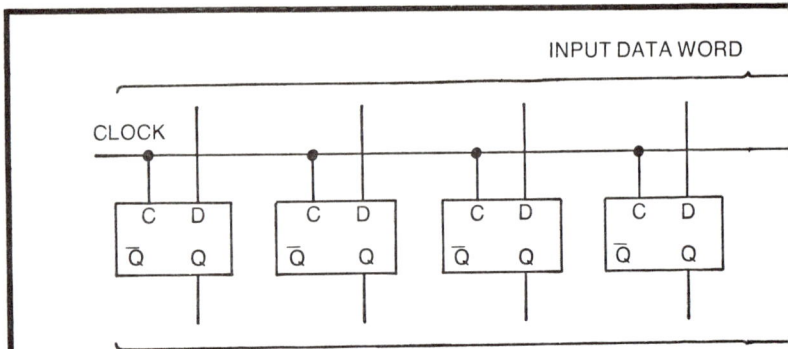

Fig. 4-26. An 8-bit data register built using eight data latches. Each of the data latches holds one bit of the 8-bit word.

The pencil and paper approach to solving this problem is serial. First, we add 7 and 8. The result is 15. The 5 is written down and there is a carry of 1. Second, we add 6 and 7 and the carry of 1. The result is 14. The 4 is written down, and again there is a carry of 1. We proceed serially through this problem, adding one column of digits at a time. If we were to solve this problem on a calculator the method is entirely different. First, we enter the number 12567. Second, we press the plus button. Third, we enter the number 35378. Fourth, we press the equals button and the answer 47945 appears. The calculator processed the addition of the two 5-digit numbers in parallel. This parallel processing is the type used by the microprocessor rather than the serial used by hand.

Microprocessors process fixed-sized groups of bits at a time. Common size groupings or words for microprocessors are 4, 8, and 16 bits. During processing a group of bits must be held at some location for the duration of the process. They are normally held in a *register*. A simple register may be no more than a sufficient number of data latches to hold the word being processed. Figure 4-26 shows eight data latches used to hold a single word. Each time the common clock line is taken high a new input-word is *strobed* into the 8-bit register. This word appears at the output of the register (one bit at each latch output) until a new word is strobed in by another clock pulse.

Registers do not have to be constructed of data latches, although this is quite common. The J-K or the D-type flip-flops make excellent registers with some special properties. Registers constructed with these flip-flops may be *cleared* (the outputs are set to all zeros) or *set* (the outputs are set to all ones). They are also immune to changes on the inputs during

64

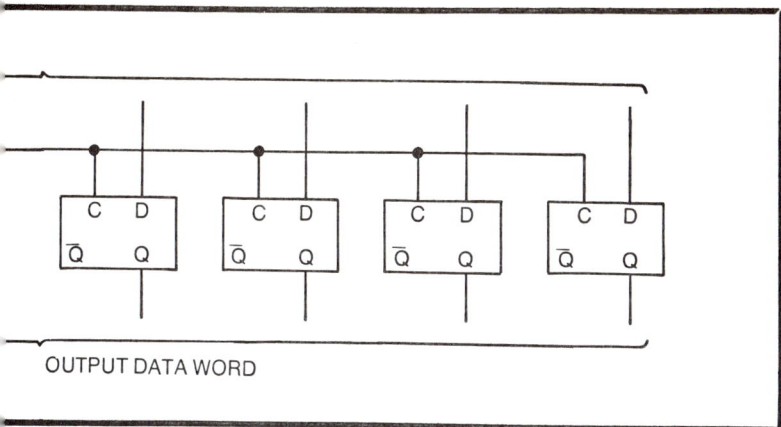

OUTPUT DATA WORD

the clock pulse. Remember the output of the simple latch changes with input changes when the clock is high.

THE SHIFT REGISTER

The simple register of the previous discussion is only capable of storing information. The *shift register* is a special form of register. The shift register can not only store information but it can also pass the information to either the right or the left.

A simple 4-bit shift register is shown in Fig. 4-27. The operational sequence of the shift register is:

1. a logic 1 is placed at the input;
2. the common clock line is taken through a complete pulse;
3. at the leading edge of the first clock pulse, Q_0 goes high in response to the logic 1 at its input at the time of the leading edge of the clock pulse. All others remain at logic 0 in response to the logic 0s at their inputs at the leading edge of the clock pulse;
4. at the leading edge of the second clock pulse Q_1 goes high in response to the logic 1 at Q_0 (the number two flip-flop input). Q_0 goes to logic 0 as the input line was logic 0 *before* the leading edge of second clock pulse. All other Qs remain at logic 0 for the same reason;
5. at each successive clock pulse the logic 1 signal is passed further down the register chain.

The operation just described is a very simple shift register. The process is called *shifting right*. This term is derived from the direction the logic one pulse goes on each

65

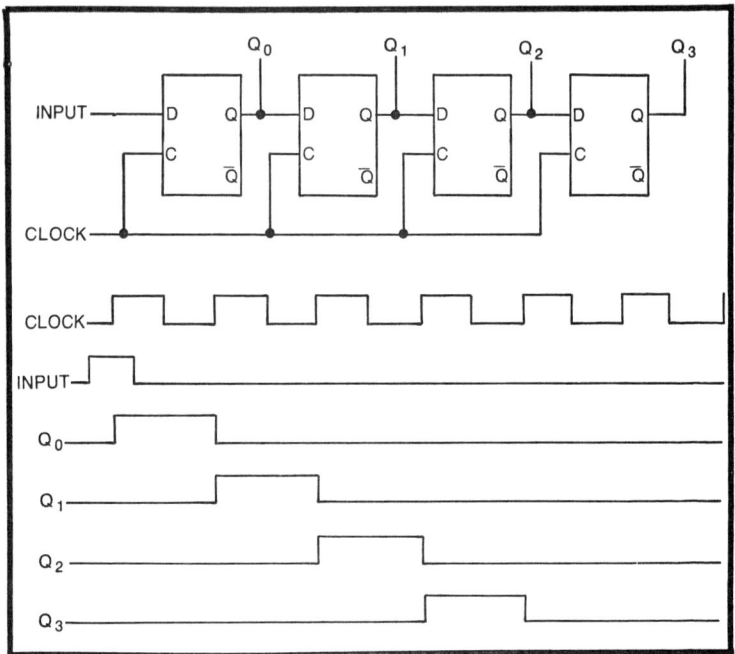

Fig. 4-27. A simple shift register. Information loaded in each stage of this shift register is moved to the stage to the right each time a clock pulse is received. The waveform diagrams show the shifting of this information.

successive clock pulse. Some of the features found on more sophisticated shift registers are:

1. shift right and shift left capability;
2. both parallel and serial inputs;
3. a circulate mode which connects the output of the last stage of the shift register to the input of the first stage;
4. clear and set capabilities.

When the shift register is used in the microprocessor, two modes may be used. *Shift* means the data is lost as it leaves the last stage of the shift register. *Rotate* means the register is in a circulating mode. The data is therefore not lost.

The shift registers found inside microprocessors are the same length as other registers in the microprocessor. Very long shift registers enjoyed some popularity as memories for a short while.

THE COUNTER

Another form of the register is the *counting register*. It is often referred to as simply a *counter*. As was noted in the J-K flip-flop discussion, a 11 condition on the J and K inputs causes the output waveform at Q to be one-half the frequency of the clock-input waveform. In Fig. 4-28 three flip-flops are connected in series so the output signal of the first is the input signal for the second. The output signal of the second is the input signal for the third. At each output the signal frequency is one-half the previous input. This effect is shown in the waveforms in Fig. 4-26.

If all the flip-flop outputs are initially set to zero and all the outputs are carefully observed after each input pulse, the table of Fig. 4-28 is created. With no pulses applied the ABC outputs are 000. With one pulse applied they are 100, with two pulses they are 010 and with three pulses they are 110. On the seventh pulse the ABC outputs are 111, and the eighth pulse causes the outputs to return to the original 000 condition.

The counter has two uses. It may be used to derive a signal which is a submultiple of some higher frequency. It may also be used to count the number of pulses since the counter was reset to a known conditon.

If the counter starts at the 000 condition and proceeds to the 100, 010, 110, etc., the counter is said to be *incrementing*, or counting up. However, the flip-flops may be rewired so they reverse this sequence. That is to say, they start at 000, proceed to 111 then to 011, 101, etc. When a counter acts in this manner it is said to be *decrementing*, or counting down. Counters are most commonly used to provide various frequencies or *timing signals* for microprocessors. However, many of the registers in the microprocessor have the capability to increment or decrement. Drawing an analogy to a counter will aid you when the terms increment and decrement are used.

THE LOGIC FAMILIES

In the course of time since the integrated circuit was introduced in the early 1960s, a number of different technologies have been used to implement digital circuits. Some have faded, some have little or no use in the microprocessor world, but some others have found extensive use with the microprocessor.

TTL

TTL is the abbreviation for Transistor Transistor Logic. It is the most common, lowest cost logic family in existence today. TTL is used primarily to make gates, flip-flops, and other logic circuits which are used as accessories to microprocessors. Such small circuits are referred to as *Small Scale Integration* (SSI). SSI is usually considered to be those

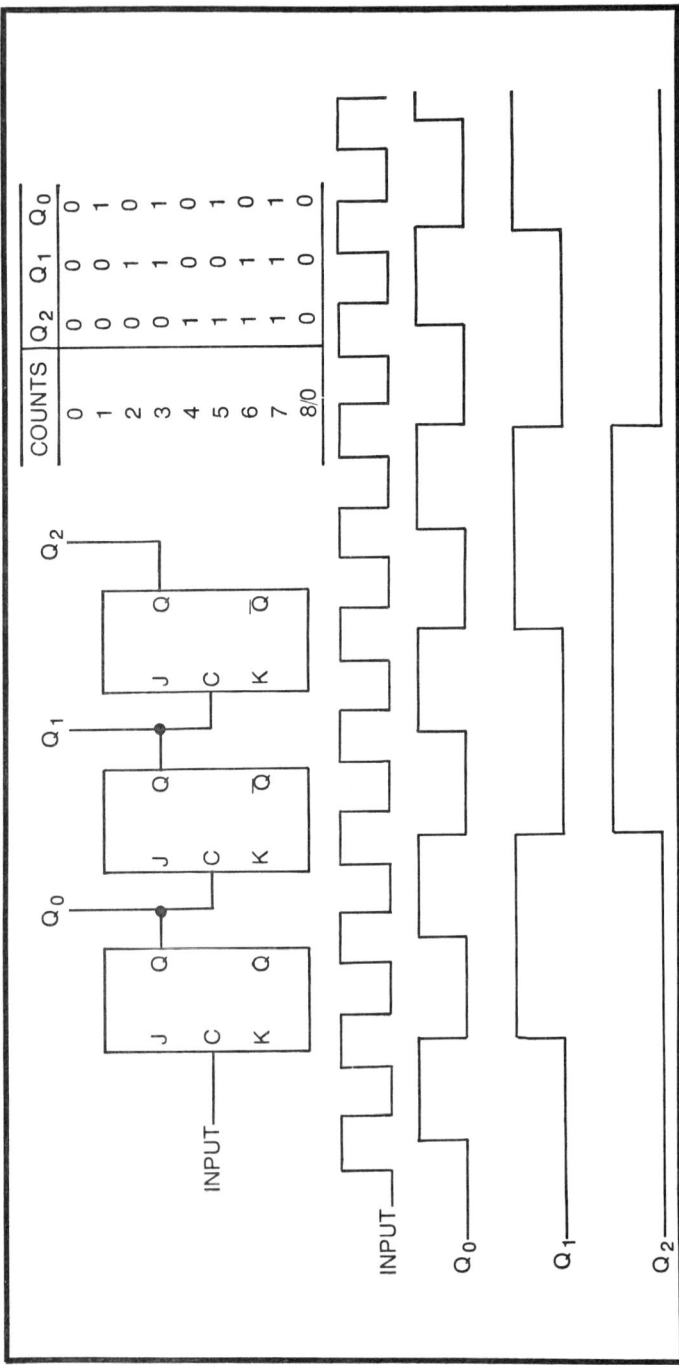

Fig. 4-28. A simple 4-stage counter. This circuit is sometimes referred to as a ripple counter as the clock signal ripples from stage to stage as the counts progress.

COUNTS	Q_2	Q_1	Q_0
0	0	0	0
1	0	0	1
2	0	1	0
3	0	1	1
4	1	0	0
5	1	0	1
6	1	1	0
7	1	1	1
8/0	0	0	0

circuits containing the equivalent of 20 gates or less. Circuits which are between 20 and 200 gates are referred to as Medium Scale Integration (MSI). Counters, multiplexers, shift registers, and decoders are common examples of MSI. Large Scale Integration (LSI) refers to integrated circuits which are sufficiently complex to require 200 or more gates. Because TTL is so common, many microprocessors are designed to be compatible with TTL circuits. The major characteristics of TTL circuits are:

1. +5 volt supply;
2. one output can generally drive ten inputs (*fanout* of 10);
3. for logic 1, an input requires at least a 2.0 volt level capable of supplying 40 microamperes;
4. for logic 0, an input requires less than a 0.8 volt level capable of sinking 1.6 milliamperes;
5. series 7400 TTL and series 74LS00 TTL are 20 to 30 MHz logic families;
6. there are well over 200 different TTL ICs available today. Almost all are SSI or MSI;
7. TTL outputs are designed to supply 0.4 volts greater signal than required by an input circuit.

MOS

Metal Oxide Semiconductor (MOS) technology is the technique which enables the semiconductor industry to produce extremely large integrated circuits. Most MOS circuits are LSI. Once LSI became practical, the microprocessor and such important accessories as memories became practical.

There are a number of different forms of MOS technologies, the two major distinctions being P-channel and N-channel MOS. The P and N refer to the positive and negative nature of the semiconductor material used to start building the IC. P-channel MOS is one of the earlier MOS technologies. Very little microprocessor work is done in P-channel MOS, although a great deal of memory and calculator work was done in P-channel MOS.

There are two major variations of N-channel MOS. One technology requires three different operating voltages, −5 volts, +5 volts and +12 volts. Other voltages are also used with this same N-channel MOS. Special versions of low threshold N-channel MOS have been developed requiring only one supply voltage. Usually this is +5 volts. Both of these N-channel technologies have some form of TTL compatability, although neither drives more than one or two TTL inputs. As the MOS N-channel technologies continue to develop, manufacturers will strive to lower the power required and to improve the speed of the ICs.

The most recent MOS technology is Complementary MOS (CMOS). Complementary indicates the logic utilizes both P-channel and N-channel construction within the same IC. The utilization of both technologies permits a radical reduction in the power used by the IC. CMOS also offers some speed improvements as well, although speed tends to offset some of the power savings. CMOS technology is producing SSI gates and flip-flops; MSI-decoders, multiplexers, and counters; and LSI memories, calculators, and microprocessors.

There are only a few CMOS microprocessors to date, but this area of semiconductor technology will grow rapidly. CMOS makes it possible to run an entire microprocessor system on a few flashlight batteries.

Chapter 5

The Microprocessor as a Central Processing Unit

This chapter looks at the microprocessor as it is used as a *central processing unit*. As has been noted earlier, many of the available microprocessors contain additional parts of the digital computer other than the central processing unit. These parts are covered in separate chapters. As you become familiar with what goes on in a generalized microprocessor, you will be able to see what parts of common microprocessor ICs are central processing units and what parts may be memory or I/O (input/output).

THE CENTRAL PROCESSING UNIT

Central Processing Unit (CPU) is used to designate a particular portion of a digital computer. Generally, it refers to the section of the computer called the "brain" or the "heart" of the computer. Today, CPU may take on an additional meaning, as it may also be used to refer to a microprocessor IC.

What is the CPU? The CPU consists of a data processing system, a number of registers to hold data, and digital logic to control the sequence of all CPU, memory, and I/O operations.

The registers are simply designated areas within the CPU where a word may be stored. Each register is assigned a name (usually in the form of a binary number) so it may be addressed by CPU instructions when the programmer wishes to store data or retrieve data from the register.

The CPU retrieves stored instructions and data words from memory. It also deposits processed data in memory. The CPU may also be connected to I/O devices, such as teletypewriters, keyboards, TV displays, etc. I/O devices permit the programmer (user) to communicate with the microprocessor. I/O devices are the microprocessor's means of communicating with the outside world. This may not always be with the programmer.

For the digital computer or the microprocessor to communicate with the outside world, the information or data from the outside world must be converted into *data words*. For example, if the information in the outside world is the position of a control which moves a figure on a TV game, the position of this control must be "digitized". This digitized information can then be accepted by the microprocessor. If the microprocessor is sending out data to move a TV game figure across the screen, the data words must first be converted to TV signals. Converting signals to data words and converting data words to special signals is done by I/O devices. In many cases the signals in the outside world are not digital but analog in nature. In such cases the I/O devices are *Digital to Analog* (D/A) or *Analog to Digital* (A/D) *converters*.

As we said earlier, the CPU is the brains of any computer, be it a large data processing machine or a simple microprocessor. The CPU has three basic functions. First, it *fetches* an instruction word stored in memory. Second, it determines what the instruction is telling it to do. Third, it executes the instruction. Executing the instruction may include some of the following major tasks.

1. Transfer of data between registers in the CPU itself.
2. Transfer of data between a CPU register and a specified memory location.
3. Performing arithmetic or logical operations on data from a specific memory location or a designated CPU register.
4. Directing the CPU to change a sequence of fetching instructions, if processing the data created a specific condition.
5. Performing housekeeping functions within the CPU itself in order to establish desired conditions at certain registers.

As mentioned earlier, a microprocessor's CPU contains a number of registers. What are these registers for, and what do they do? The register is a place within the CPU where a single word may be stored. In many ways, it is exactly like one word of the microprocessor's memory. Commonly, the microprocessor has two or more *working registers* where data may be stored while in process. In addition to *data registers,* there are usually three to five other registers within the CPU which manage such housekeeping functions as:

1. keeping track of the current memory location (address) where the next instruction word is stored;
2. keeping track of the current memory location (address) where any data transfers from CPU registers to or from the memory are to occur;
3. holding the current instruction while it is being executed so the CPU can continually refer to this instruction;
4. holding data being transferred with memory or with an I/O device;
5. storing indications of special conditions created by an arithmetic or logic operation on data being processed by the CPU.

Registers

In the next few sections we shall take a more detailed look at the uses for a number of registers common to most microprocessor's CPUs.

As each register is described, a figure highlighting that register shows its place in a common microprocessor CPU. Although this CPU is hypothetical, it should give you a good picture of how the particular register is connected to other parts of the CPU, what its size is, and whether it supplies, receives, or supplies and receives data.

The Accumulator and ALU. The primary use of the *accumulator* and the *Arithmetic and Logic Unit* (ALU) is in data processing. The accumulator and ALU are highlighted in Fig. 5-1. All data is placed into the accumulator for processing; then, once it has been processed, it is returned to the accumulator. The normal path for data being placed in the accumulator is through the ALU. By means of the ALU, data transferred into the accumulator may be:

1. added to the data already in the accumulator (binary addition);
2. subtracted from data already in the accumulator (binary subtraction);
3. shifted one or more bits (binary digits) to the right or to the left;
4. logically ANDed to the data already in the accumulator;
5. logically ORed to the data already in the accumulator.

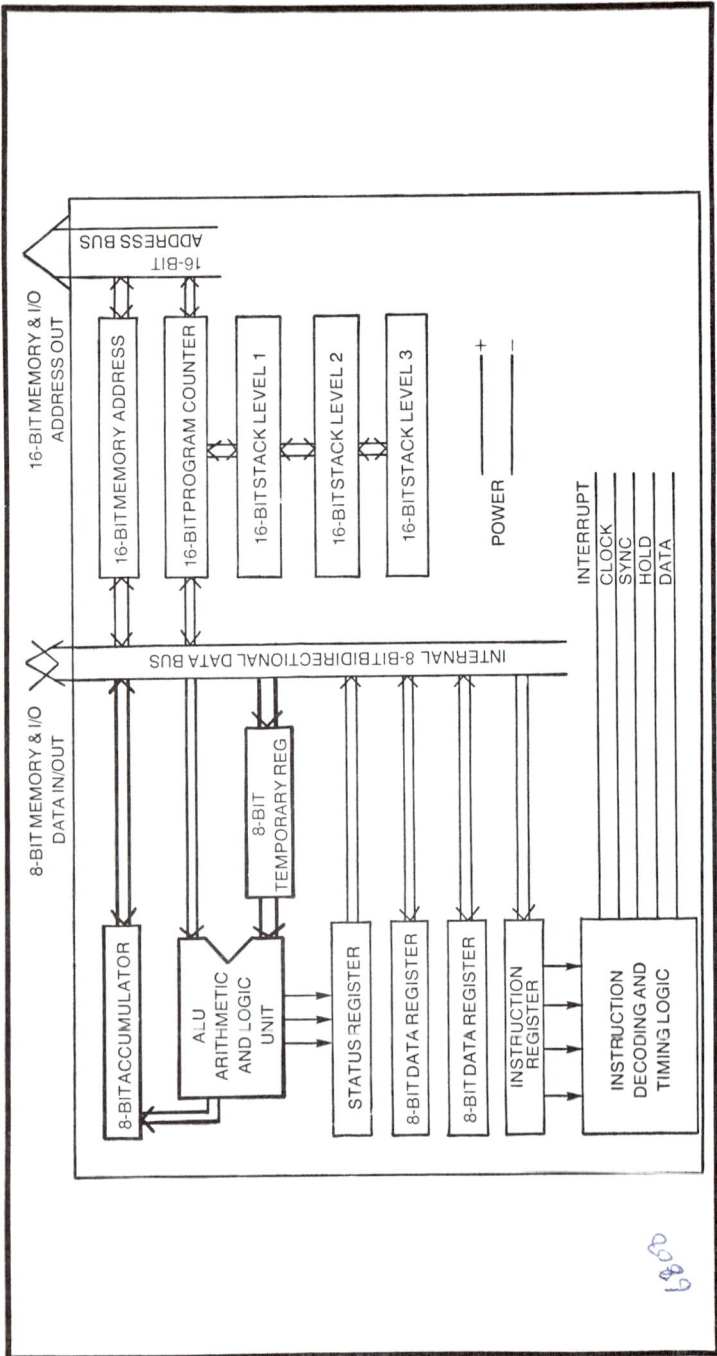

Fig. 5-1. A typical microprocessor CPU shown with the accumulator and the arithmetic and logic unit highlighted.

Depending on the microprocessor, there may be other manipulations which the CPU may be instructed to perform on data entering or leaving the accumulator.

Some microprocessors have only a single accumulator, others may have two or more. Often microprocessors with only a single accumulator have a number of simpler storage registers. These simpler storage registers avoid transferring to and from memory data that is to be imminently processed in the accumulator. Memory data transfers are much slower than transferring data between CPU registers.

The length of the microprocessor's accumulator (and the length of any other of the microprocessor's data registers) is generally the same length as the microprocessor data word. For example, an 8-bit microprocessor has an 8-bit accumulator. A few exotic 8-bit microprocessors use a two byte (16-bit) accumulator. This makes some arithmetic functions (those which tend to overflow a small accumulator) simpler.

When thinking of the functions of the accumulator, keep its name in mind. The accumulator *accumulates results of operations* on the data being processed. Some microprocessors have a temporary register as a second ALU input. These registers temporarily hold data during the ALU/accumulator process.

The Program Counter. The program counter, highlighted in Fig. 5-2, keeps track of the memory location containing the next program step the CPU is to FETCH and then EXECUTE. At the beginning of a CPU's FETCH/EXECUTE cycle, the binary number (value) of the program counter is connected to the memory address lines. The addressed memory word is the next one in the instruction sequence. The word is fetched from this memory location and used as the microprocessor's next instruction. Once an instruction is fetched from memory, the program counter is incremented. Incrementing the program counter increases its value by 1. The incremented program counter now contains a binary number that addressed the *next* instruction to be used by the microprocessor. Therefore, while the microprocessor is executing the current instruction (just fetched) the program counter is *pointing* to the *next* instruction.

The program counter may be considerably longer than the processor data word. The program counter must address any word of memory conceivably connected to the micro-processor. For most microprocessors, this is any one of 65K (65536) words. Addressing 65K requires a 16-bit address word ($2^{16} = 65536$), or two bytes. Most microprocessors do not use

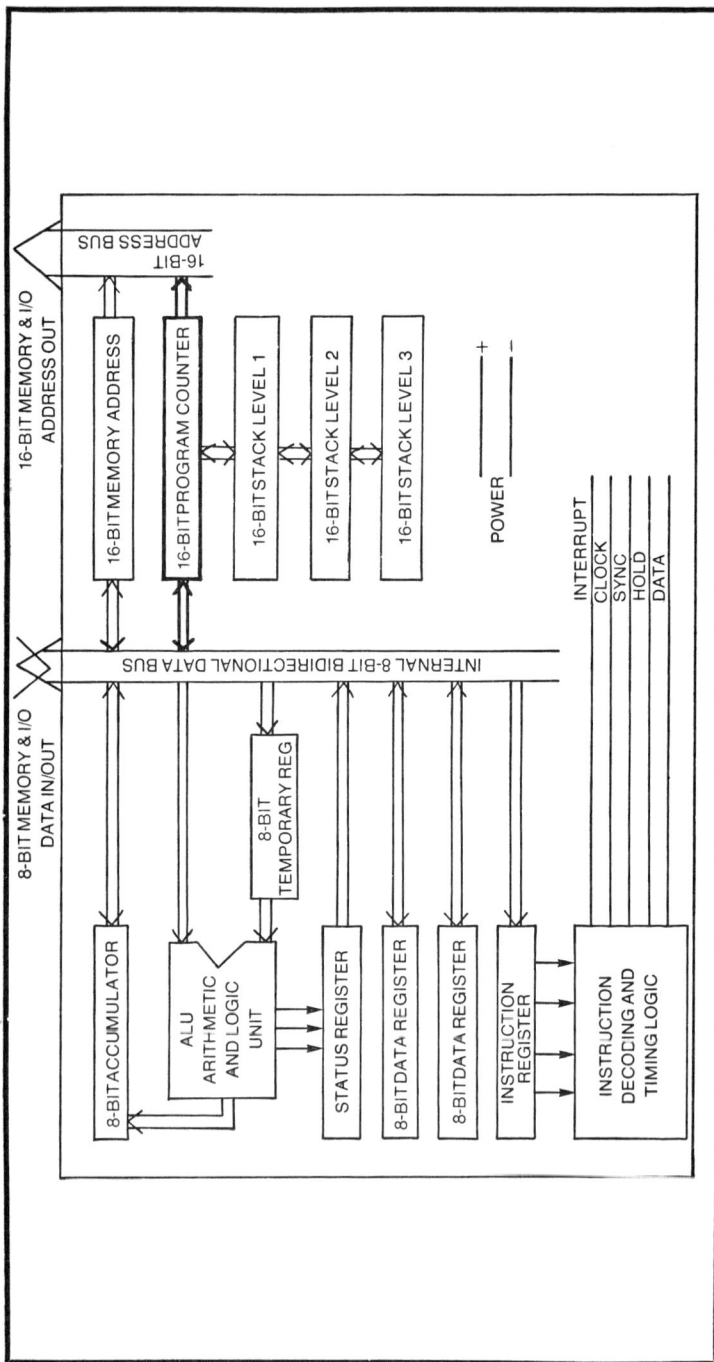

Fig. 5-2. A typical microprocessor CPU shown with the program counter highlighted.

16-BIT MEMORY & I/O ADDRESS OUT

16-BIT ADDRESS BUS

16-BIT MEMORY ADDRESS

16-BIT PROGRAM COUNTER

16-BIT STACK LEVEL 1

16-BIT STACK LEVEL 2

16-BIT STACK LEVEL 3

POWER
+
−

INTERRUPT
CLOCK
SYNC
HOLD
DATA

INTERNAL 8-BIT BIDIRECTIONAL DATA BUS

8-BIT MEMORY & I/O DATA IN/OUT

8-BIT TEMPORARY REG

8-BIT ACCUMULATOR

ALU ARITH-METIC AND LOGIC UNIT

STATUS REGISTER

8-BIT DATA REGISTER

8-BIT DATA REGISTER

INSTRUCTION REGISTER

INSTRUCTION DECODING AND TIMING LOGIC

all the possible memory. However, this capability must be there in case the microprocessor is used with the maximum memory, or in case the small memory is placed at any location.

Program counter operation is simple. Its only operation is to increment. If the execution of the instruction requires the number in the program counter to be completely modified, the program counter is loaded with an entirely new value. An 8-bit microprocessor with a 16-bit program counter requires two data moves to completely change the contents of the program counter. The program counter contents are supplied in two halves. A data transfer instruction brings in one 8-bit data word (the low byte) which replaces the least significant half of the program counter valve. A second data transfer brings in a second data word (the high byte) which is the most significant half of the program counter value.

When the program counter is temporarily loaded with a new binary number (value), the programmer may wish to return to the original program sequence after a few instructions at the new location. This is often the case when the programmer wishes to use a short sequence of instructions over and over again at various points in the main program (a *subroutine*). When this is the case, the binary number contained in the program counter may be placed in a special storage area called a *stack*. The new binary number is then loaded into the program counter. When the programmer wishes to return to the original program sequence, the old binary number for the program counter is recalled from the stack.

The Stack and the Stack Pointer. The stack highlighted in Fig. 5-3 saves the binary number in the program counter when the program counter number is changed. As noted earliler, often the programmer wishes to frequently use a short program at another location. Such short programs are called subroutines. For example, in the course of solving a problem, a programmer may need to multiply one number by another at seven or eight different points within the program. Unfortunately, multiplication is not a normal instruction for a CPU. Therefore, the programmer must write a short routine (program) which multiplies two designated numbers. Repeating the multiplication routine in the main program each time the programmer needs to multiply two numbers takes time and memory space. It is simpler to direct the computer to utilize a single routine stored in a different area of memory. To utilize this subroutine, the current binary number in the

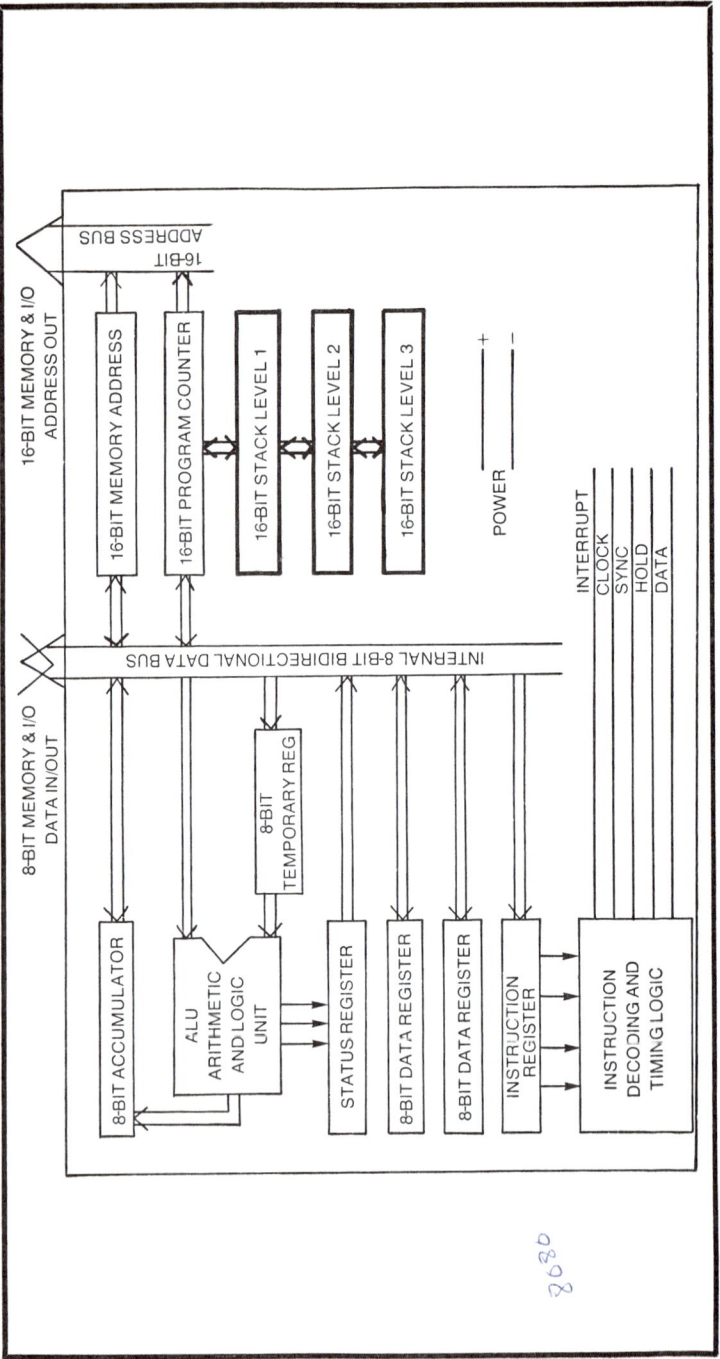

Fig. 5-3. A typical microprocessor CPU shown with a 3-level stack highlighted.

8680

program counter must be stored so the microprocessor can return to the current problem once the multiplication is complete. A new binary number representing the beginning of the multiplication subroutine is inserted in the program counter. When the multiplication is complete the programmer wishes to continue with the next step in his program. Therefore, the old binary number for the program counter is taken from the stack and placed back in the program counter.

Thus, it can be seen that the object of the stack is to save the program counter so the program may continue where it left off when it went to do a subroutine. To do this, the original program counter must be saved. There are two methods with which this is accomplished in modern microprocessors.

The simplest stack consists of a few additional registers identical in length to the program counter. If the program calls for a subroutine at a different location, the new binary number representing the new memory location is loaded into the program counter. The old binary number representing the memory address for the current sequence of program instructions is PUSHED onto the stack. When the subroutine is complete, the old binary number for the program counter is POPPED from the stack. This is to say, it is recalled from the register it was stored in, and placed back in the program counter. The CPU can now continue to process instructions in the normal sequence.

Often a subroutine is required within a subroutine. Therefore, stacks may be more than one level deep, permitting the program to have a number of subroutines and then successively return to the original program sequence.

Stacks operate on a *first in last out* basis. This is illustrated in Fig. 5-4. The program counter contains the binary number we shall call A. A subroutine is required, starting at memory location B. A is placed on the stack and B becomes the binary number in the program counter (Fig. 5-4B). A second subroutine, starting at memory location C, is called before subroutine B is complete. Binary number B is PUSHED onto the first level of this stack and binary number A is PUSHED onto the second level of the stack. This is shown in Fig. 5-4C. Figure 5-4D shows the situation after the subroutine starting at memory location C is finished. Binary value B is POPPED from the stack into the program counter to finish the subroutine started from memory location B. Binary number A, representing the point at which the original program was broken away from its sequence, is now moved to the top of the stack. When the subroutine which started at memory B is finished, binary value A is POPPED from the stack into the

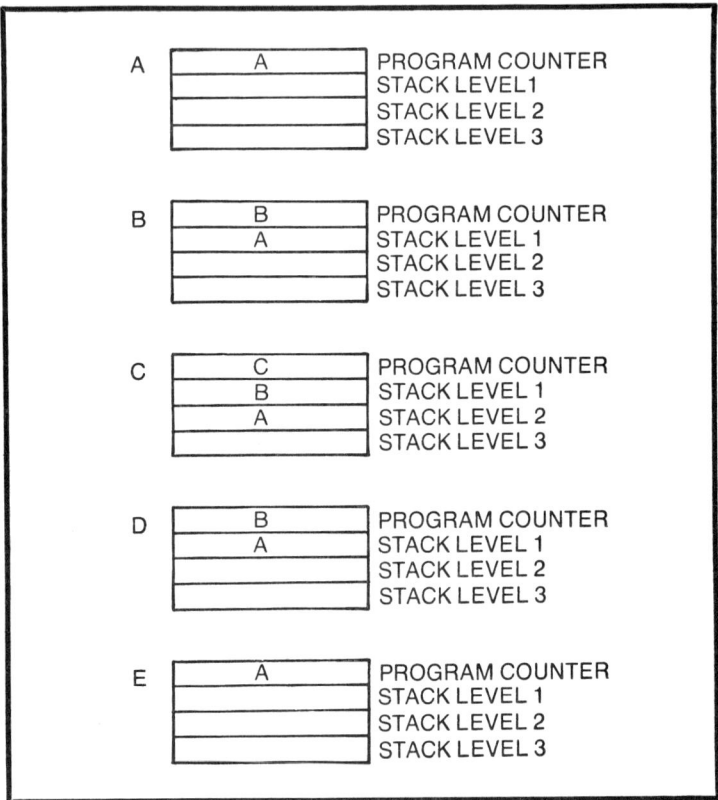

Fig. 5-4. A 3-level stack illustrating the first out principle.

program counter, as shown in Fig. 5-4E. Note that binary number A, representing the point in which the program was broken from its original sequence, was the *first* into the stack and the *last* out.

A hardware stack is limited by the number of registers in the stack. If there are only three registers in the stack, the program can only handle four interruptions before the original value of the program counter is lost. If a fifth interruption occurs the value of the program counter (representing the very first interruption now stored at the bottom of the stack) is pushed out of the stack and completely lost. Hardware stacks typically run three to seven levels deep. Although the ability to service seven interruptions within interruptions seems to be quite sufficient, this is not always the case, especially for microprocessors controlling complicated processors. These may have many outside routines which must interrupt the current sequence of operation.

A more complicated but more versatile form of stack does not use internal microprocessor registers for the stack. The actual stack storage is in the microprocessor's main memory. A single register called the *stack pointer* is used to indicate the *current stack address* on memory. This scheme is not as fast as the hardware stack. It requires time-consuming memory transfers each time an address is PUSHED onto or POPPED from the stack. This form of stack, however, gives the programmer an unlimited stack. All the programmer must do is ensure the external stack does not write over an area of memory being used for data storage or an area of memory containing a sequence of program instructions.

The stack pointer then becomes another 16-bit CPU register. Again, the stack pointer must be 16 bits, as it must be able to address the full 65K of memory that could be associated with the microprocessor, even though it is highly unlikely all 65K are used. External stacks have additional uses. They may be used to save the value of all CPU registers including the value of the stack pointer itself if a situation which causes CPU failure is impending. Such a situation, for example, might be a power failure. In order to make such an external stack feasible, the microprocessor must be equipped with memory which does not fail (forget) when power fails.

The Instruction Register. The *instruction register* (highlighted in Fig. 5-5) stores the binary word fetched as an instruction during the decoding and execution portions of the CPU cycle. The contents of the instruction register may not be changed except by calling a new instruction.

The instruction-register length depends on the microprocessor. Instruction registers vary in length from a few bits to registers as long as the processor data word itself.

The instruction-register output continuously drives the digital logic which controls the microprocessor. This instruction timing, decoding, and control logic determines the required sequence of events to carry out the instruction just fetched and placed in the instruction register. Most microprocessors are *microprogrammed.*

Microprogramming means the microprocessor instruction decoding operates like a small version of a microprocessor itself. As the microprocessor goes through the fetch and execute cycles, the microprogram logic goes through a series of fetch and execute cycles of its own. It looks up the proper control sequence in an internal *Control Read Only Memory* (CROM) to carry out the instruction in the instruction register. Microprocessors are microprogrammed to carry out their instructions simply because this is the easiest way to implement the microprocessor logic.

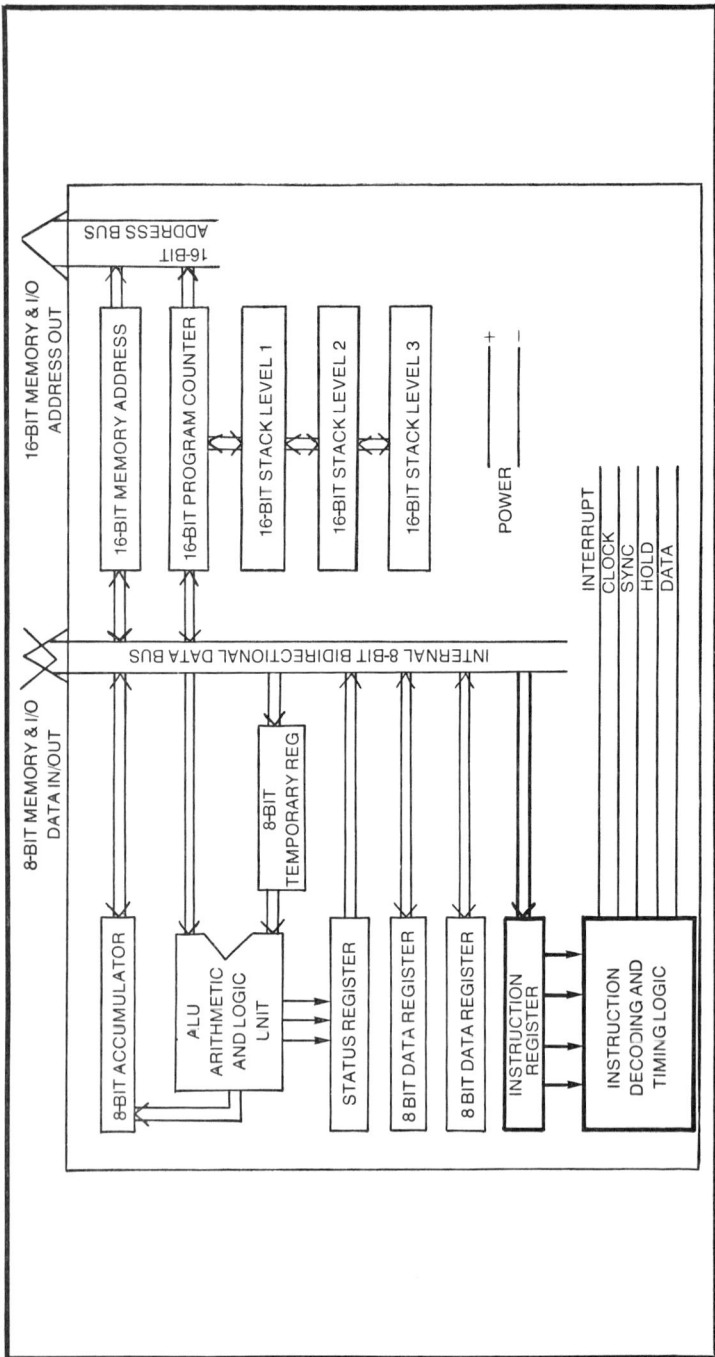

Fig. 5-5. The instruction register highlighted here stores the binary word fetched as an instruction during the decoding and execution portions of the central processing unit cycle.

82

The Memory Address Register. The *memory address register* (Fig. 5-6), contains the current address of the memory word being used as data work space. The memory address register addresses memory whenever the CPU calls for a memory data transfer instruction to be executed. At that time, the binary number contained in the memory address register is used to address memory.

Unlike the program counter, the memory address register does not automatically increment once its contents have been called. Incrementing or decrementing (increasing or reducing the binary value of the counter by one) of the memory address register must be done by the programmer. For example, the programmer may leave the memory address register at a binary number that points to one particular word of memory for a number of fetch/execute cycles of the CPU. During these CPU cycles, the binary value contained in the memory word at that particular memory location may change a number of times as the CPU passes through the various fetch and execute cycles.

If the programmer desires, the memory address register may be incremented or decremented each time a memory data transfer occurs. If the programmer increments the memory address register for every data transfer, the data is loaded in sequential memory locations. This is often done to generate a *file* (a file is an area in memory containing a sequence of data stored for use at a later time.)

The length of the memory address register determines the maximum size memory the microprocessor may address. By far the most common size is the 16-bit address. This allows addressing 65K words of memory. Although, as pointed out before, few microprocessors use the full 65K words, this capability is built into most microprocessors. A few microprocessors limit their maximum memory size to either 32K or 16K words of memory.

When the microprocessor has a 16-bit memory address register and an 8-bit data word, the memory address register may actually be two separate registers. Often these are referred to as *HI byte* and *LO byte* memory address registers. When the memory address is broken into HI and LO bytes, the LO byte addresses one of 256 words ($2^8 = 256$). HI byte addresses 256 blocks of memory (each block containing 256 words.) Simple multiplication shows 256 blocks, each containing 256 words, results in the total memory of 65,536 words, or 65K words.

Depending on the particular microprocessor, there may or may not be a carry from the LO byte to the HI byte. The word

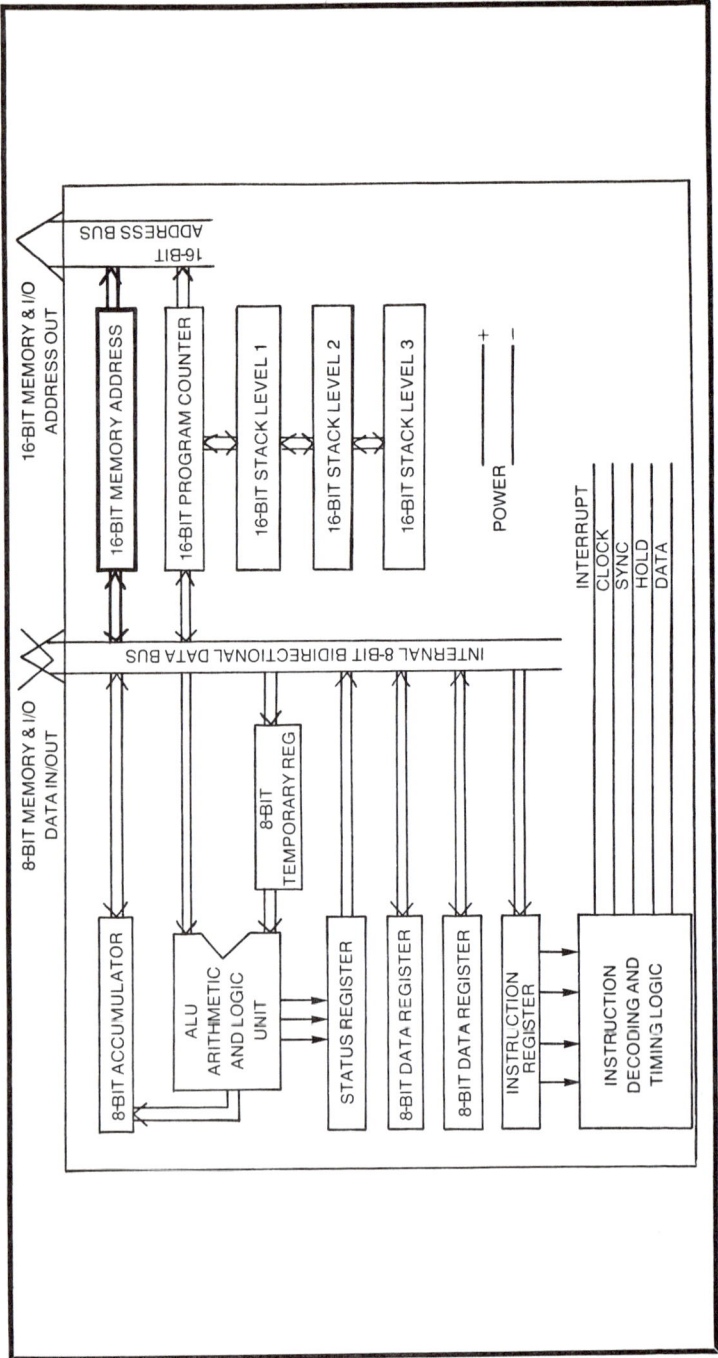

Fig. 5-6. Highlighted here is the memory address register. It contains the current address of the memory word being used as data work space.

"carry" is used here in the same manner as you expect from simple arithmetic. For example, when the LO byte register is incremented from 11111111 to 00000000, the HI byte should increment by one, as a carry is generated by the LO byte. This is just like going from 999 to 1000. If the microprocessor does this automatically, no extra effort is required by the programmer. Without *automatic carry* between the HI and LO bytes, the programmer must test the LO byte each time it is incremented. When a 00000000 is detected in the LO byte, the HI byte is incremented.

The binary number in the memory address register is always under the programmer's control. To provide the initial starting point, the register must be loaded with a binary number representing the first location for memory data transfer instructions. If the memory address register contents are to be changed, there must be an instruction in the program to accomplish this change. The memory address register may be loaded from memory, or from other registers, one byte at a time. Separate instructions may load the HI and LO bytes, or a single instruction may load the LO byte, then the HI byte.

The Status Register. Most frequently the *status register* records results of data processing in the accumulator or associated registers. For example, if two numbers are added in the accumulator and their sum is greater than the accumulator can hold, an *overflow* or simple *arithmetic carry* results. One status-register bit is reserved to indicate such an arithmetic over-flow occurred. Once the bits of the status register are set by an operation, a second instruction directs the microprocessor to examine the status-register contents. If necessary, the program sequence is changed to follow a new course based on the status-register results.

For example, a data word may be brought into the accumulator and incremented. Each time this occurs the next instruction tests a status-register bit. A one in this bit indicates the accumulator became zero on the execution of the last instruction. When a test of the status register records a zero accumulator on the last instruction execution, the program counter is loaded with a new binary number. This starts the program at a new location in memory, altering the program execution sequence.

Some of the common condition bits in a status register are:

1. CARRY—an accumulator arithmetic overflow occurred on execution of the last instruction;
2. ZERO—all bits in the accumulator were zero after the last instruction executed;

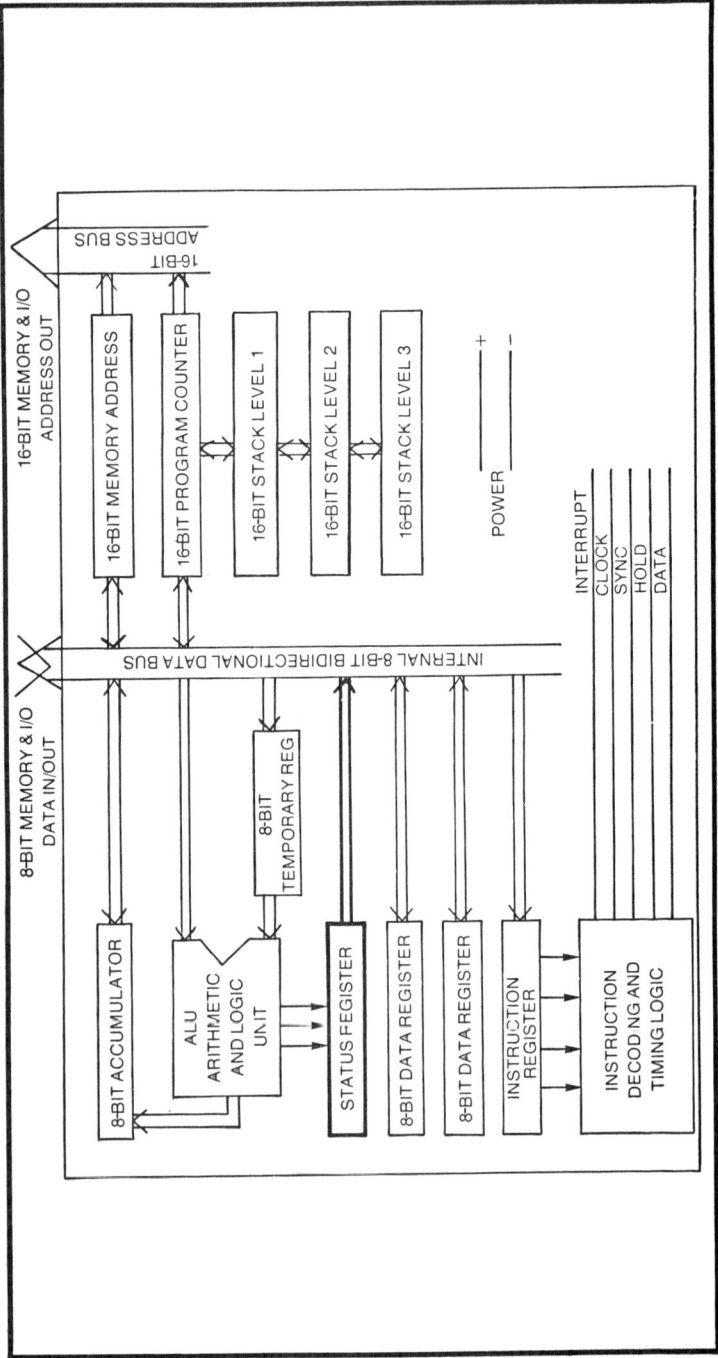

Fig. 5-7. This status register mostly records results of data processing in the accumulator or associated registers.

3. NEGATIVE—a logical 1 was left in the most significant bit of the accumulator after the last instruction executed;

4. INTERMEDIATE CARRY—an arithmetic carry was generated between the fourth and fifth bits of the accumulator;

5. INTERRUPT MASK—the interrupt port is turned on;

6. OVERFLOW—both an arithmetic carry and a sign carry occurred in two's complement arithmetic (a subtraction technique);

7. PARITY—the number of ones in the accumulator is not even following execution of the last instruction.

Most microprocessors do not use all the above *status flags*. However, the first three are common to virtually all microprocessors. The status register is very important to microprocessor applications. One of the fundamental capabilities of a digital computer, and therefore a fundamental capability of the microprocessor, is the ability to make decisions based on the data being processed. The status register is used to flag the program that a particular situation has occurred and that a decision must be made.

CONNECTING THE MICROPROCESSOR TO OTHER DEVICES

Placing the microprocessor in an integrated circuit package creates certain problems. The single biggest problem is bringing out all the required signals from the limited number of pins available on an integrated circuit package. ICs come in 8-, 14-, 16-, 18-, 22-, 24-, 28-, and 40-pin packages. Reviewing all the connections required for an ordinary 8-bit microprocessor, we find many packages are entirely too small. Of course, the larger the package is, the more expensive it is.

Bidirectional Data Bus

To keep cost as low as possible, some special connections help reduce the pin requirements. One of the methods used to conserve pins is the use of the *bidirectional data bus*. The bidirectional data bus consists of eight lines (on an 8-bit or byte oriented microprocessor) carrying data into and out of the microprocessor. The use of a bidirectional data bus reduces the data pins from 16 to 8. Because the data bus is bidirectional, there is no need for a separate set of 8 pins for the data transmitted out of the microprocessor. The use of the bidirectional data bus generates a requirement for a control signal to tell external devices if the data bus is transmitting (sending the data out of the microprocessor) or receiving. This signal uses one pin and, therefore, the end result is not an eight-pin saving, but a seven-pin saving.

Direct Memory Access

In some special applications it is desirable to have an external device rather than the microprocessor supply address and data information to the memory. An example of this situation is Direct Memory Access (DMA). Under DMA the memory may be loaded rapidly from an external mass storage device as shown in Fig. 5-8. DMA is covered in detail in Chapter 6. To apply external address and data, the microprocessor must stop processing. It goes into a *hold* state. Also, the address and data lines must be switched off at the microprocessor. This keeps conflicting information from appearing on these lines. Switching the address and data lines off is referred to as placing them in the *tri-state* condition. Microprocessors have an input line to command the tri-state condition. The microprocessor completes its current instruction and then gives a TRI-STATE ACKNOWLEDGE signal on another pin.

Data on the bidirectional bus is not always intended for memory. It may, for example, be intended for an I/O transfer. Therefore, memory must be told when to read and when to write. Usually memory read/write control is a single pin on the microprocessor.

The Interrupt Line

The *interrupt line* is a common microprocessor input. If the microprocessor is busy solving a problem, for example, and a device on the outside urgently needs its services, the external device INTERRUPTS the microprocessor. There are a number of different kinds of interrupts found on various microprocessors. The exact handling of an interrupt depends on the microprocessor. Interrupts are covered in more detail in Chapter 7. If the microprocessor is to have interrupt capability there must be an interrupt input pin. Some microprocessors have multiple interrupt lines, which require more than one input pin.

The Reset Line

When the microprocessor is initially turned on, the program counter assumes a binary number which is a completely random value. As a matter of fact, so do all other registers in the microprocessor, such as the status register and the accumulator. The program counter must be set to some known binary number in order to start executing the program at the beginning point in memory. A *reset* line places

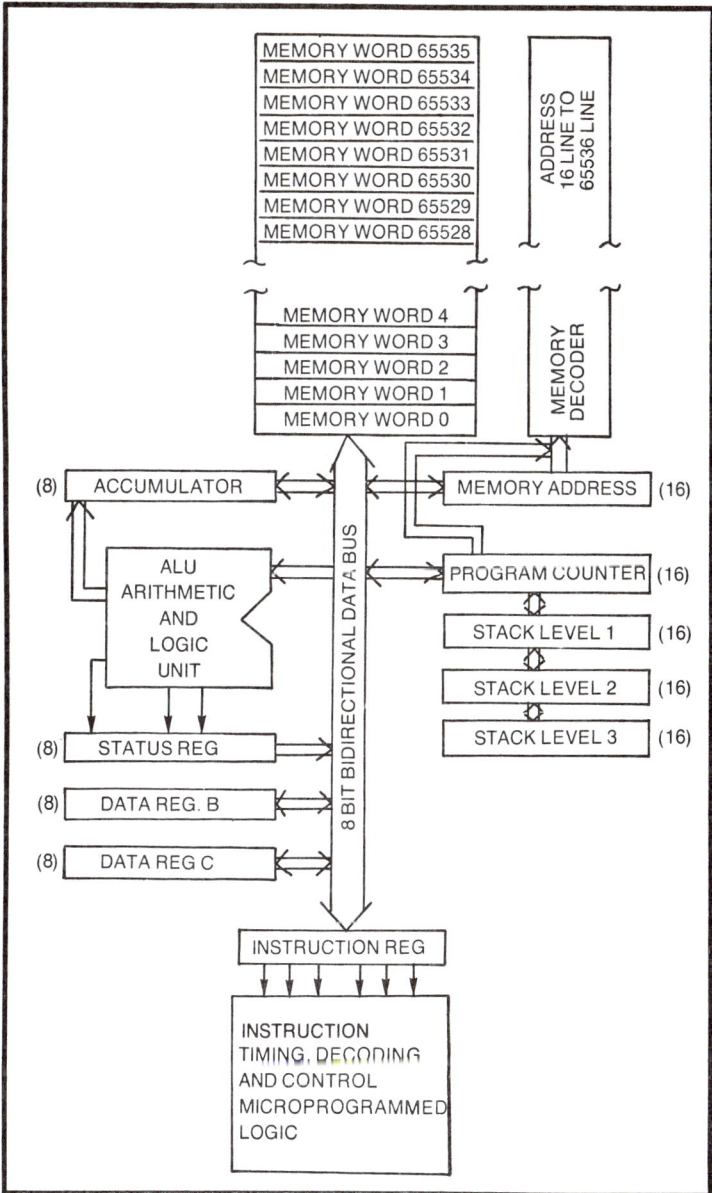

Fig. 5-8. Direct memory access allows rapid transfer of external mass storage data.

Table 5-1. Typical 8-Bit Microprocessor Signal Connections.

SIGNALS	NUMBER OF PINS
A. Memory Address Lines	16
B. Data Input/Output Lines	8
C. Clock Input	2
D. Interrupt Input	1
E. Reset	1
F. Memory Read/Write Control	2
G. Input/Output Read/Write Control	2
H. Data Bus Direction	1
I. Positive Power Supply (B+)	1
J. Power Supply Return (Gnd)	1
K. Tri-State Control	1
L. Tri-State Acknowledge	1
TOTAL	37

the program counter at an initial value. The accumulator and the status register are usually placed at all zeros on a RESET command. The reset value of the program counter is not always all zeros, but it is always the same binary number for every reset command. The programmer can always start the program at the memory location which occurs on reset, or store a jump instruction at the reset location. The microprocessor then jumps to the program starting program.

Table 5-1 is a list of signal and power connections one might expect to find on an 8-bit microprocessor.

The power lines in the table are given as B+ and ground. Many microprocessors use multiple power lines such as −5 volts, +5 volts, +12 volts, and the ground or return line. Each power line requires a separate pin.

These 37 signals are only a generalized list. A more detailed list can be found on individual microprocessor data sheets. As one can see, microprocessors are almost forced into the 40-pin ICs. In fact, most microprocessors make full use of all 40 pins, and additional pins are welcome.

A few microprocessors carry the bidirectional data bus further. The data bus does not simply carry bidirectional data but also carries the memory address information or status information. Of course, this even further reduces the required number of IC pins. The address or status signals are first placed on the bus, followed by data signals. This method requires a control signal so devices outside the microprocessor can tell which signal is on the bus. Using this technique and others, a few microprocessors fit 16-, 18-, and 24-pin IC packages.

Chapter 6

Memory

What is *memory*? As we have learned earlier, memory is where instructions and data are stored. Up to this point, little has been said about how the program and data words are stored. This chapter covers the fundamentals of memory devices used with microprocessors.

The chapter of basic logic reviews building of storage registers with flip-flops. Obviously, one way to build a memory is to use row upon row of flip-flop storage registers. Indeed, this is a fairly common method of creating memories. From somewhere in the past you have probably heard the term *core memory*. Sometimes this is simply referred to as *core*. Core memory makes use of the magnetic properties of certain materials. Large resisters can be made using these magnetic flip-flops, and this has been the main type of computer memory for many years.

There are two basic forms of memory. The one most commonly used for general purpose microprocessor memory is *Random Access Memory* (RAM). RAM permits the user to write and read words in any memory location once the location is addressed. *Read Only Memory* (ROM) permits reading data from the addressed location. It does not permit writing new data into the location. Needless to say, ROM is not used for data manipulation, but it is very convenient for storing frequently used programs.

Although core memory played a significant role in the development of the computer, microprocessors primarily use semiconductor memory. The same technologies leading to the microprocessor lead to semiconductor memories. Core

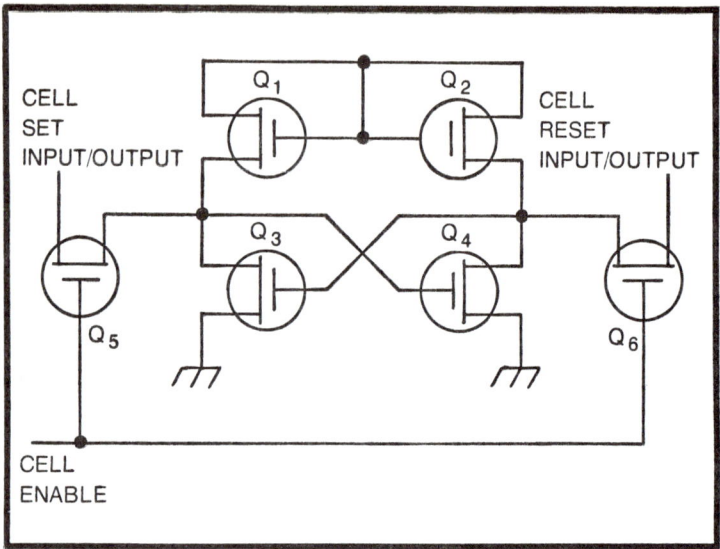

Fig. 6-1. A six transistor static memory cell. The transistor Q_3 and Q_4 form a simple RS flip-flop which is the basic storage element. Transistors Q_1 and Q_2 serve as load resistors for Q_3 and Q_4. Transistors Q_5 and Q_6 connect the cell input/output signals to external circuitry.

memory is quite inexpensive in very high volume. However, for the relatively small memories used with microprocessors, semiconductor memory is generally the least expensive. Semiconductor memory prices are falling rapidly; they are rapidly becoming the major technology for large computer memories as well.

SEMICONDUCTOR RANDOM ACCESS MEMORY

Two semiconductor technologies are commonly used to build memory ICs. The most common is Metal Oxide Semiconductor (MOS). *MOS memories* are the lowest cost, use the least power, and store the most bits. The MOS memory is built using the MOS transistor. Semiconductor memories are also built using the bipolar transistor. MOS transistor construction is far simpler than bipolar transistor construction. This is one reason MOS memories are cheaper, and easier to build than *bipolar memories*.

Bipolar memories are expensive, use more power, and have less storage capacity than MOS memories, but they do offer some advantages. Bipolar memories are extremely fast. In fact, bipolar memories can be at least ten times faster than their MOS counterparts. Bipolar memories are built using Transistor Transistor Logic (TTL) and Emitter Coupled Logic

(ECL) technologies. ECL bipolar memories are extremely fast. They are normally employed in large computers or special microprocessor applications where extreme speed is of value and cost is not particularly important.

When discussing MOS memories, two terms immediately surface. They are: *static* and *dynamic*. Static and dynamic describe two different ways the MOS transistor is used to build a memory. Figure 6-1 is a simple diagram of a single static MOS cell. This construction is the simplest flip-flop. The memory is static because once the flip-flop is set (or reset), it remains in that state until an electrical signal changes it.

The many transistors required to build static memories make them slightly less desirable from a size and cost standpoint than dynamic memories. The MOS dynamic memory of Fig. 6-2 relies on a completely different property of the MOS transistor. The MOS transistor input is an extremely high impedance. This means it draws virtually no current from the circuit driving it. Because it draws little or no current, a logic 1 may be represented by the charged capacitor. The length of time the charge remains on the capacitor before decaying depends upon how closely the MOS transistor input approaches infinite impedance. Obviously, no MOS transistor is perfect. Therefore, to store information on the capacitor for a long time, the charge must be *refreshed* at regular intervals.

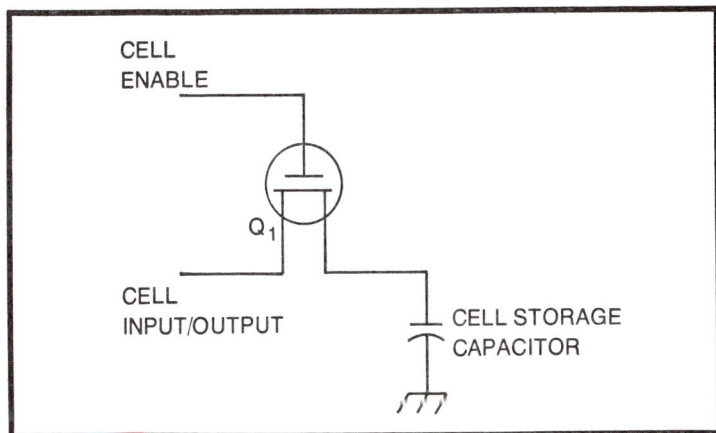

Fig. 6-2. A single transistor single capacitor dynamic memory cell. A logic 1 is stored as a charge on the cell storage capacitor. A logic 0 is a discharged capacitor. Q_1 is used to connect the capacitor to the input/output line. Note the dynamic memory cell is considerably simpler than the static cell, but the charge on the capacitor must be periodically refreshed.

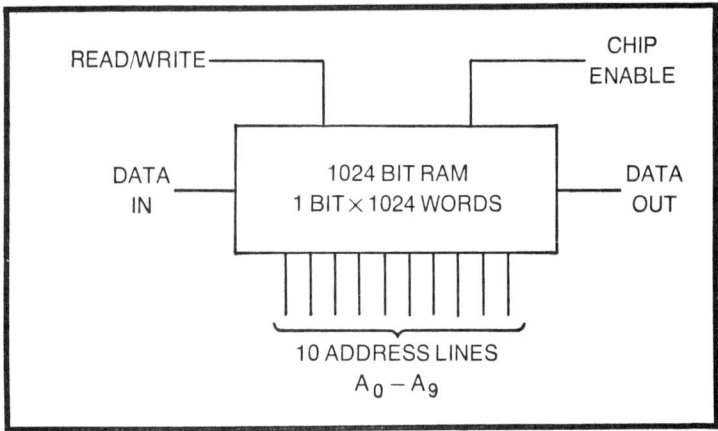

Fig. 6-3. The 1,024 bit memory. Each individual memory cell is addressed by the appropriate binary number on the address lines. Once addressed (and enabled), the read/write line determines whether data is written into the addressed cell or read from the addressed cell.

The smaller the capacitor, the more frequently the circuit must be refreshed. *Refreshing* the dynamic memory 300 times per second provides an effective compromise between the nonproductive effort of refreshing the memory and making the storage capacitors as small as possible. This reduces the circuit cost and increases the number of bits on a particular size integrated circuit.

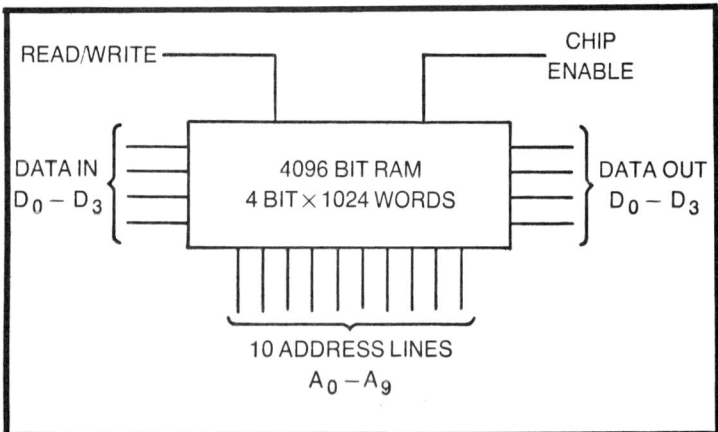

Fig. 6-4. The 4,096 bit memory. Each bank of four memory cells is addressed by the appropriate binary number on the address lines. Once addressed (and enabled), the read/write line determines whether data is written into the four addressed cells or read from the four addressed cells.

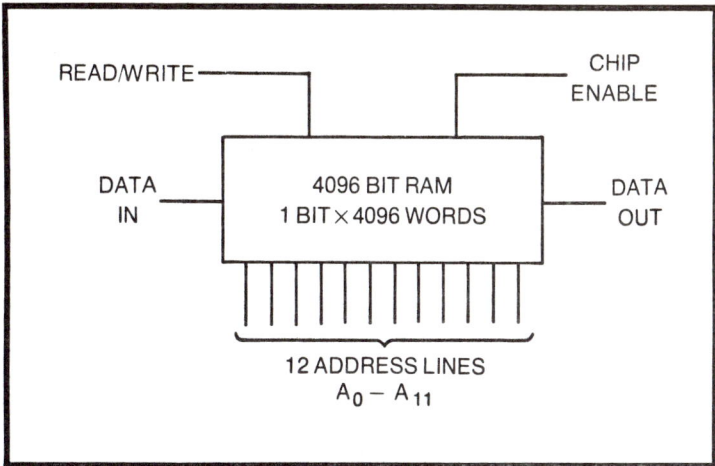

Fig. 6-5. A 1K word memory with 4 bits per word. Note that the chip enable line is used to select the 1K block of addresses used by this memory.

Because the dynamic memory is simpler than the static memory, (compare Fig. 6-2 to Fig. 6-1) larger memory ICs are usually available as dynamics first. For example, the 1K (1.024 bit) dynamic memory preceded the development of the 1K static memory by approximately 1 year. In a similar manner, the 4K dynamic memories were introduced in early 1975. The 4K static memories were introduced in early 1977. Current technology is pointing toward both 16K and 65K memories.

For most microprocessors, we want memories to be organized in 8-bit words. Figure 6-3 shows three available organizations of 1K and 4K memory ICs. These organizations are used with dynamic and static memories. The 1K-by-1 bit configuration of Fig. 6-3 requires eight ICs to build a 1K word memory with eight bits per word. The 1K-by-4-bit IC of Fig. 6-4 requires two integrated circuits to build a memory with 1,024 8-bit words. Figure 6-5 shows a 4K-by-1 chip. If there are sixteen bits in a memory word, either sixteen-1K-by-1 or four 1K-by-4 chips are required. Memories requiring less than four bits per word must be built with 1K- or 4K-by-1 chips. Figure 6-6 is a simplified schematic of a 1,024 word memory with four bits per word. The memory uses four $1,024 \times 1$ memory ICs. There are 12 address lines, but only 10 are used to select one of the 1,024 words. The other two lines drive a 2-line to 4-line decoder. The user may install one connection from the decoder output to the chip enable line. With this connection the memory address will be in the following ranges:

JUMPER	MEMORY ADDRESS RANGE
1K	0−1,024
2K	1,024−2,048
3K	2,048−3,072
4K	3,072−4,096

This technique can be expanded to place the 1K of memory anywhere from 0 to 65K. Memory ICs are available in lengths other than 1K and 4K. As noted earlier, 16K dynamic memories are being introduced at this time and earlier developments produced 256- and 512-bit memories.

Fig. 6-7 shows the cell selection process for a typical memory. Notice the memory cells are addressed by two decoders. The input word is broken in half. For example, a 1K word memory requries 10 address bits ($2^{10} = 1,024$). The 100 address bits are broken into two 5-bit segments. Each drives a 5-line-to-32-line decoder. The low-order bits drive the column select decoder and the high order 5-bits drive the row select decoder. The resultant 32-by-32 grid identifies one of the 1,024 memory cells. If the concept is expanded to 64 by 64 (two 6-line to 64-line decoders), the 64-by-64 grid gives 4,096 points. This is the construction of a 4K memory.

OTHER RANDOM ACCESS MEMORIES

Although semiconductor RAM is most commonly used with microprocessors, the reader should be aware of other technologies. Some of these technologies are only used in very special microprocessor situations, and others will be used in large microprocessor systems when the technology fully emerges.

As noted earlier, the core memory was the mainstay of computers for many years. Core memory or magnetic memories have a major advantage. They are *nonvolatile*. A *volatile* memory loses the stored information when the power is turned off. All semiconductor memories fall into this category.

As the nonvolatile characteristics of core memories are very appealing, an effort has been made to integrate the magnetic memory. The result of this effort is new technology called *bubble memories*. Bubble memories are very large and nonvolatile. At the present time, however, bubble memory speeds are quite low. The speed of a typical semiconductor memory may be in the area of 100 to 450 ns (0.0000001 to 0.00000034 second). The bubble memory speed may be more in the area of 1 ms (0.001 second). Current work in the field of bubble memories is on pointing memory units able to store 512K bits. Therefore, at the current time, bubble memories

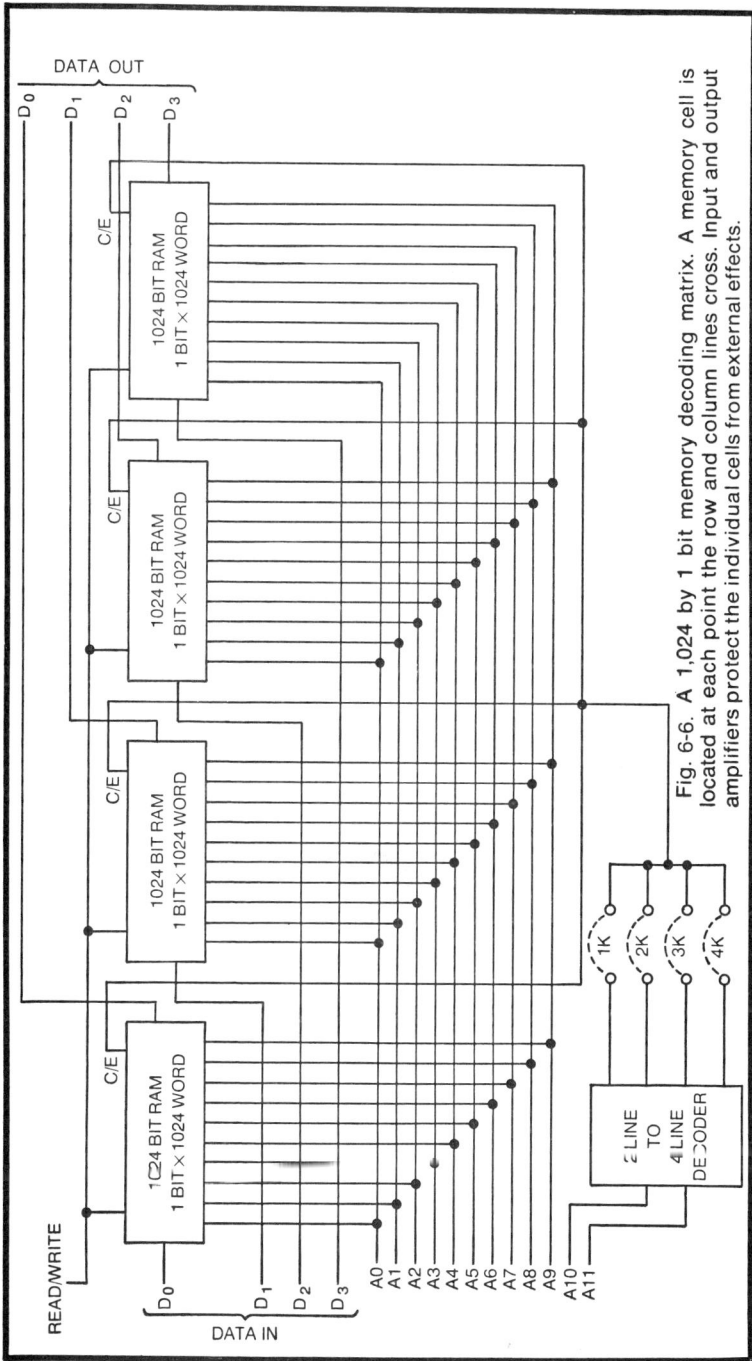

Fig. 6-6. A 1,024 by 1 bit memory decoding matrix. A memory cell is located at each point the row and column lines cross. Input and output amplifiers protect the individual cells from external effects.

97

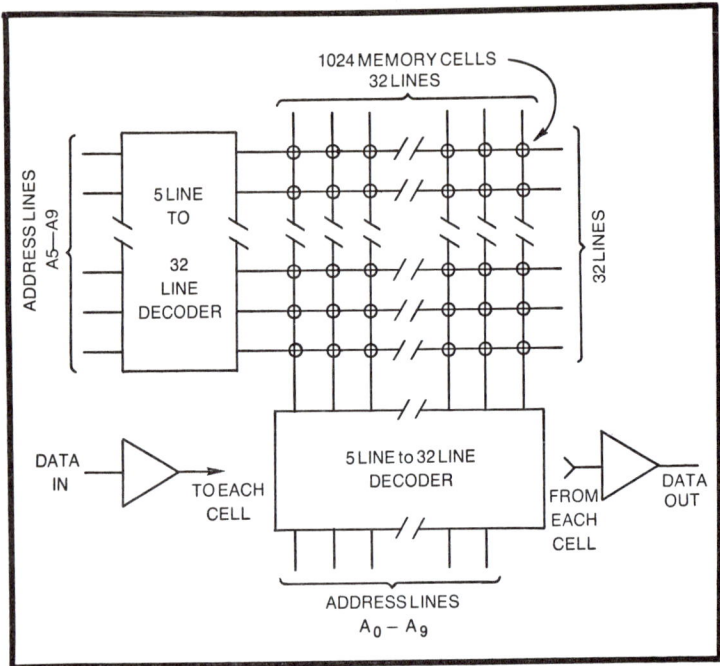

Fig. 6-7. Simplified schematic of a 1,024 word memory with 4 bits per word.

seem to be headed toward mass storage, novolatile, rather slow, applications.

CCD MEMORIES

Another semiconductor technology becoming quite popular is CCD. CCD stands for *Charge Coupled Devices*. CCD memories offer low cost and the ability to integrate many bits on a small chip. Once again, the penalty for this large integration is a slower access time. The speed of CCD memories is like the bubble memory speed. CCD memories are also volatile, but use very low power and, therefore, can be supported by batteries through long power outages.

READ ONLY MEMORIES

Read Only Memory (ROM) plays an extremely important role in the world of microprocessors. Many microprocessor applications require the microprocessor to use a single fixed program. However, this program is utilized over and over. For example, a microprocessor is used to control a stop light. The program operating the stop light conducts all the timing and determines when the red, green, and yellow lights should be turned on. It may even modify the timing with traffic flow. However, this is the only program the microprocessor ever does. There may be some minor amounts of data stored, such as timing information or traffic flow information. For this purpose, a very small amount of RAM is required. However, this may be no more than a few bytes. The main program is stored in ROM. The advantage of the ROM is cost and nonvolatility. That is, if power is lost, the ROM does not forget its preprogrammed information.

Figure 6-8 shows a simple diode ROM. When a diode is in place, the memory generates a logic 1 when the location is addressed. When the diode is missing, the ROM generates a logic 0. This concept is integrated to build large ROMs. Once again, row and column selects are used to decode the proper address.

There are a number of different forms of ROMs available. One of the most common ROM's for high volume production is the *mask programmable ROM*. The ROM contents are specified by the user and the semiconductor manufacturer changes the photographic negative used to etch away the metal interconnecting various parts of the integrated circuit. Once this mask has been etched to a particular customer's configuration, the program stored in the ROM is permanent and may only be changed by etching a new mask.

As second form of ROM is the *fusable link* or *field programmable ROM*. In its initial state, the fusable link ROM

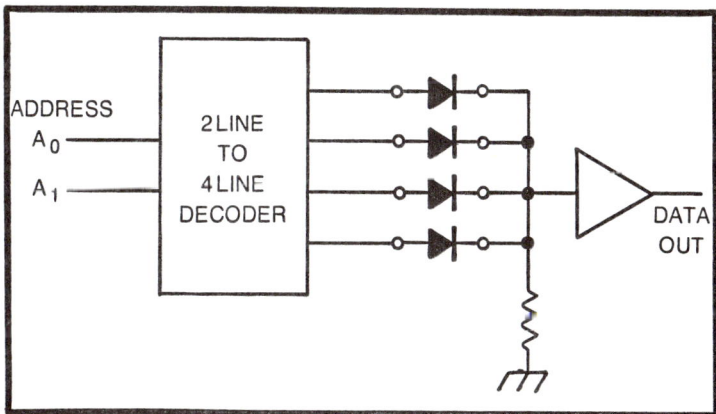

Fig. 6-8. The 4-bit diode ROM. When the decoder selects a diode, a logic 1 is generated if the diode is in place. If the diode is removed, a logic 0 is generated. Unwanted diodes are "blasted" out.

contains a logic 1 for every possible bit. However, the field programming "blasts" the fuses at the desired locations to produce the desired bit pattern. Once a ROM has been "blasted" it is permanently encoded. The field program ROM costs more than the mask programmable ROM; however, there is no masking charge. This technique, therefore, permits the user to make program modifications on a few ROMs. This ROM is found in many microprocessor circuits where only a few units are built with one particular program.

Such ROMs are often referred to as PROMs, which stands for *Programmable Read Only Memories*. Very frequently PROMs are used to cover an additional form of memory, more correctly referred to as an EPROM, or *Erasable Programmable Read Only Memory*.

The erasable programmable read only memory, as its name implies, may be programmed to a 1-bit pattern and later erased and programmed with a new bit pattern. There are two common techniques for erasing EPROMs. The most common and oldest of the technologies is the *ultraviolet erasable*. The ultraviolet EPROM uses a special quartz lid to cover the integrated circuit. When the IC is exposed to ultraviolet light, the "blasted" zeros "heal". A newer technique is healing with an electrical current. These EPROMs are sometimes referred to as *electrically alterable memories*.

EPROMs often find their way into microprocessor circuits in the same manner as PROMs. In fact, these two terms are often utilized interchangeably. Both the ultraviolet and the electrically alterable read only memories are accessible to the sophisticated experimenter. Quite a few of the ultraviolet erasable PROMs are available on the surplus market today.

DIRECT MEMORY ACCESS

Direct Memory Access (DMA) is a technique often employed in both large computers and microprocessors when the user desires to transfer large quantities of information from an external device to or from the main processor memory. For example, having a microprocessor containing 16K words of memory, and wishing to place the entire contents of this memory on a *floppy disc*, the speediest way to perform this transfer is by DMA. In the DMA mode, the microprocessor is disabled. The memory addressing is taken over by the device making the DMA transfer. The data is supplied by the addressing device or by the addressed memory location. Once the device has completed the transfer, control is returned to the microprocessor.

During DMA, memory information may be transferred at close to the maximum main memory read/write rate. This is many times faster than it is possible for the microprocessor to fetch the data from memory, place it in an appropriate register, and then output the information to a particular I/O port. DMA is quite common with magnetic tape and floppy discs. It is also used to supply information to a graphics terminal, where a great deal of information must be presented in a very short time to a television-like screen.

MEMORY TYPES

Memory may be divided into two basic types. *Main memory* and *mass storage*. Main memory is directly addressable by the microprocessor. This memory contains the program controlling the microprocessor and serves as storage for the data being processed. Microprocessor main memory is usually semiconductor RAM or ROM. Mass memory or *bulk storage* is used to store programs not presently being processed or to contain large quantities of data not immediately required. Mass storage devices are covered in Chapter 8.

Chapter 7

I/O Ports or "Communicating With the Microprocessor"

Up to this point we have discussed moving and processing data within the microprocessor and its memory. However, the best microprocessor in the world equipped with the most memory is of no use if the information cannot be moved in and out of the microprocessor. In order to do this, we must communicate with the microprocessor. Communicating with the microprocessor is done with *input/output (I/O) ports*. I/O ports permit the microprocessor to send data words to the outside world or to input data words from the outside world.

There are two basic forms of I/O connections: *parallel* and *serial*. Obviously, each has its own special application. This chapter deals with the fundamentals of parallel and serial I/O connections, *I/O addressing*, and a system by which a device in the outside world tells the microprocessor it needs to be serviced, called *interrupts*.

PARALLEL I/O CONNECTIONS

Parallel I/O connections are used when the microprocessor must communicate with a local external device at fairly high data rates. Parallel I/O connections are moderately simple. The basic word in the microprocessor is processed in a parallel format so moving a parallel word to or from an I/O port is very natural.

Often the parallel I/O port requires some form of storage. The storage usually takes the form of an 8-bit data latch on an 8-bit microprocessor. The data must be stored at the I/O port because the microprocessor executes the I/O instruction very rapidly (it executes all instructions very rapidly). If the microprocessor is to output a data word to a particular I/O port, the data word may be presented to the I/O port for only a few microseconds. By the use of an 8-bit data latch, the word may be stored at the output port long enough for the external device to make use of it.

Likewise, an external device may supply an input word. It is advantageous to let the external device leave the word at an 8-bit data latch at the input port so the microprocessor may input the word when it is ready.

Often, additional information must accompany reading and writing of data to an I/O port. For example, the device at the outside world must be told the data is available at an output port; and in turn, the outside world device must tell the microprocessor via the output port it has received the information and is ready for additional information. The lines communicating this information are called *handshake lines*. Similar handshaking lines are required on input data lines.

Figure 7-1 shows a simplified schematic diagram of a parallel I/O port. This particular port has three 8-bit data latches. The first data latch stores parallel information coming into the microprocessor. The second data latch stores parallel output information. The third data latch is called a *status latch*. Each bit of the I/O status latch controls an I/O handshaking function. Frequently the I/O service program sets or reads appropriate status latch bits prior to reading or writing data to the input and output latches.

Parallel input and output lines are normally Transistor Transistor Logic (TTL) signals. However, some special parallel I/Os and circuits contain power transistors capable of handling high current loads such as relays and small motors.

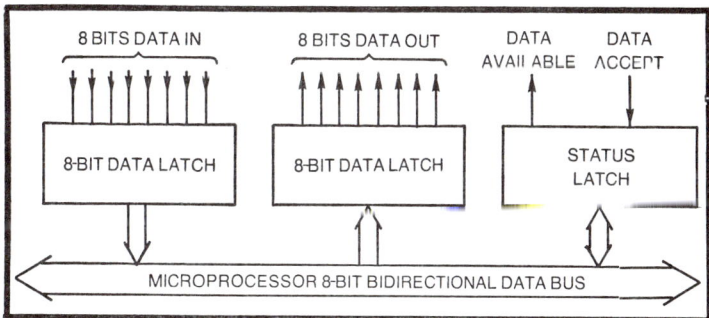

Fig. 7-1. A parallel data port. This port has eight latched input lines, eight latched output lines and a status register.

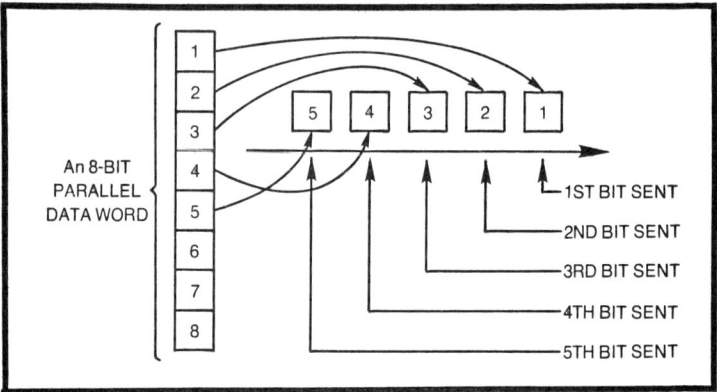

Fig. 7-2. Converting parallel information to serial information. Each bit of the parallel data word is sent on the serial line, one at a time.

Parallel interfaces are used for such applications as high speed paper tape reader/punches, magnetic tape drives, high speed printers, controlling instruments, reading data from instrumentation, and process control inputs and outputs.

SERIAL I/O CONNECTIONS

Many I/O devices use *serial transmission* to communicate with the microprocessor. Serial communication is chosen because the microprocessor can communicate with a remote device by sending data over a single pair of wires. Parallel communications require sending data over 8 or 16 pairs of wires.

Data words in the microprocessor are parallel in nature. Therefore, to transmit data in serial form, the microprocessor parallel data words must be converted to a serial data word. In a serial transmission, each bit of a parallel data word is transmitted one bit at a time. The first bit is sent on the serial line first, followed by the second, third, etc., until the eighth bit is sent. Once the eighth bit of the data word is sent, a new data word may be sent, again, one bit at a time. See Fig. 7-2.

Receiving serial data is accomplished in the same manner. Eight data bits are received one at a time after the start bit is received. A stop bit (or bits) signals that all the data has been received.

Because there are no handshaking lines to tell the microprocessor when data is coming, the system is called *asynchronous*. This means there is no separate synchronizing signal sent. In order to identify the bits in a serial word, a convention has been established. Prior to sending any data bits, a *start bit* is sent, a short burst of logic 1 indicating data transmission is to start. The start bit is followed by the eight data bits. At the end of the eighth data bit, two logic 1s are sent indicating an end to the data transmission. These are the *stop bits*. The length of time required for a start bit, data bit, or stop bit is always identical.

As can be seen, the simple 8-bit data word is now 11 bits long. If the data is sent at the rate of 10 characters (words) per second, and 11 bits are required to transmit a character, the data is sent at the rate of 110 bits per second. This *data transmission rate* is called *110 baud*. Serial data transmission is now limited to 110 baud. Higher baud rates, such as 150 baud, 300 baud, 600 baud, 1200 baud, 1800 baud, 2400 baud, 4800 baud, and 9600 baud are used. However, at these higher baud rates, the convention changes from one start and two stop bits to one start bit followed by one stop bit. The two forms of the serial data word are diagrammed in Fig. 7-3.

THE UART

The *Universal Asynchronous Receiver Transmitter* (UART) is a special integrated circuit developed to convert parallel microprocessor information into serial information, including start and stop bits. The UART also receives serial information and converts this serial information into a parallel data word for the microprocessor. The UART block diagram is shown in Fig. 7-4.

The basic logic element of the UART is the *shift register*. The shift register is used to convert parallel words to serial words and serial words to parallel words. When converting a parallel word to a serial word, the shift register is loaded with the parallel word. The shifting process then begins and the serial information at the output end of the shift register is the UART output. When receiving data, the single line is the shift

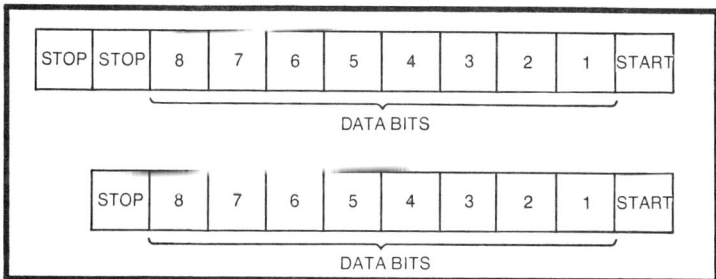

Fig. 7-3. The two forms of a serial data word. The 11-bit serial word is used at 110 baud and the 10-bit serial word is used at high baud rates.

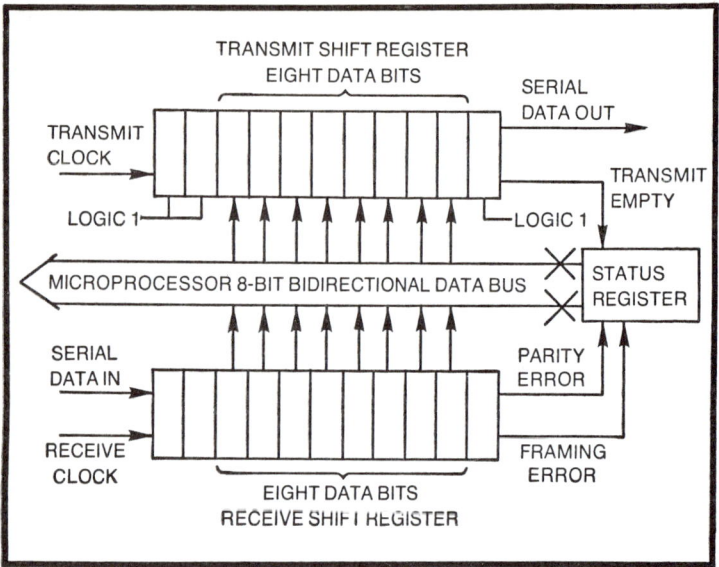

Fig. 7-4. The UART. Parallel data words from the microprocessor are converted to serial bit streams by the transmit shift register. The receive shift register inputs a serial bit stream and transfers the 8-bit bits to the microprocessor. The status register supplies control information.

register input. After the shift register completes 11 (or 10) shifts, the eight data bits are transferred to the microprocessor in parallel form. The shift register clock signal is synchronized by the start bit. Proper synchronization of the received and transmitted data depends on maintaining a constant and known baud rate.

In addition to the *input* and *output shift registers*, a *status register* provides the microprocessor with appropriate signals indicating the UART receive and transmit conditions. Some common *status word conditions* are: *transmit buffer empty, receive buffer full, parity check, stop bit error*, and *framing error*.

THE 20 mA LOOP

The *20mA loop* is one of the most common methods of transmitting serial digital information. The serial logic signals are transmitted by means of *current pulses* instead of voltage pulses. Current pulses are chosen because long transmission lines frequently have uncontrolled amounts of resistance. The uncontrolled resistance on long transmission lines causes voltage pulses to have an unknown amplitude at the receiving end. However, because current is always the same everywhere in a circuit, a 20 mA pulse at the input results in a 20 mA pulse at the output, regardless of line resistance.

THE EIA RS-232 INTERFACE

When slightly more sophisitcated serial communications are involved, a special serial communications interface defined by the Electronic Industries Association (EIA) is used. The EIA RS-232 standard defines a serial signaling system using voltage pulses. A logic 1 is defined as a voltage pulse greater than $+3$ volts, and a logic 0 is defined as a voltage pulse greater than -3 volts. In additon to defining a transmit and receive pair of wires, the EIA standard also defines a number of handshake lines. These lines permit the serial communications apparatus to answer a telephone, connect *modems*, momentarily slow down the transmission of data, and perform other similar duties. Most sophisticated terminals, such as the video terminal, have both EIA RS-232 and 20 mA serial transmission capabilities.

ASCII

American Standard Code for Information Interchange, *(ASCII)*, usually pronounced Askey, is a uniform code designed for the serial and parallel transmission of numbers, letters, and other characters. ASCII utilizes eight data bits. The first 7 data bits define a possible 128 characters ($2^7 = 128$). A table of the ASCII characters and their binary, octal, and hexidecimal equivalents is given in Appendix B.

The 128 characters represent all possible combinations of 1s and 0s for the first 7 bits. The eighth bit is called a *parity bit*. See Fig. 7-5. Parity is not required and may or may not be sent at the user's discretion. Parity is an error checking technique. There are two forms of parity, called *even parity*

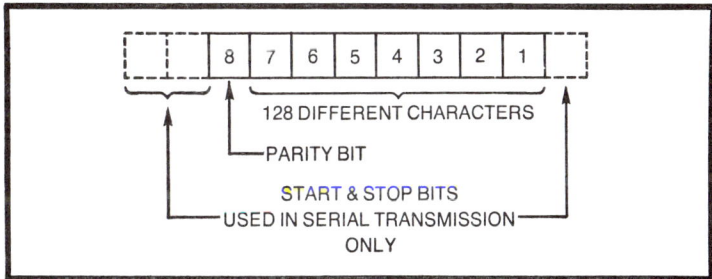

Fig. 7-5. The 8-bits of the ASCII data words. 128 different characters are represented by the first seven data bits. The eighth bit is an error checking bit (see text).

and *odd parity*. Even parity ensures the total number of logic 1s transmitted as data is even. The parity bit is sent as a logic 1 or a logic 0, to create an even number of ones. If even parity is sent, and an odd number of 1s are received, a parity error is indicated. The data must be re-sent to ensure error free transmission. Odd parity simply ensures an even number of logic 0s. Most UARTs are capable of generating and testing for parity.

When ASCII characters are sent in a serial transmission, they are preceded by a start bit and followed by stop bits. Parallel ASCII transmission is supplemented by the appropriate handshaking lines. In summary, ASCII simply assigns a 7-bit number to each of the 128 possible characters which might be used.

ADDRESSING THE I/O PORT

We have discussed both serial and parallel I/O connections for the microprocessor. In fact, the serial connection may be regarded as special device connected to a parallel I/O port. But how does the microprocessor know which device is to be serviced if more than one I/O device is connected? How does the microprocessor decide it is to read or write to an I/O device rather than a memory location?

Each I/O device must have a unique address just as each memory location is assigned a unique address. Micro-processors handle I/O addresses in two different ways. The simplest method of handling I/O devices is to assign the I/O device a memory address. Once the I/O device is assigned a memory address, this location may not be used for memory. The microprocessor does not recognize the difference between an I/O device and memory. Therefore, the user must know which memory addresses are assigned to I/O devices. When the program is to transfer information to or from an I/O device, the appropriate memory address must be called. The advantage of this sytem is common instructions for memory and I/O transfers. It has the disadvantage of limiting the memory size, at least by the number of I/O devices connected.

Other microprocessors differentiate between I/O devices and memory. These microprocessors generate special status signals indicating the address and data signals are to be directed to an I/O device rather than memory. The advantage of this system is to allow a large number of I/O devices to be connected to the microprocessor without reducing the total number of memory locations the microprocessor can use. Of course, this system requires a special instruction to address I/O devices.

Microprocessors which specially address I/O devices can use memory locations as I/O device addresses if the user wishes. However, if the microprocessor uses memory locations for I/O devices, then this system must always be used, as there is no provision for separate I/O devices. Figure 7-6 diagrams both methods of I/O addressing.

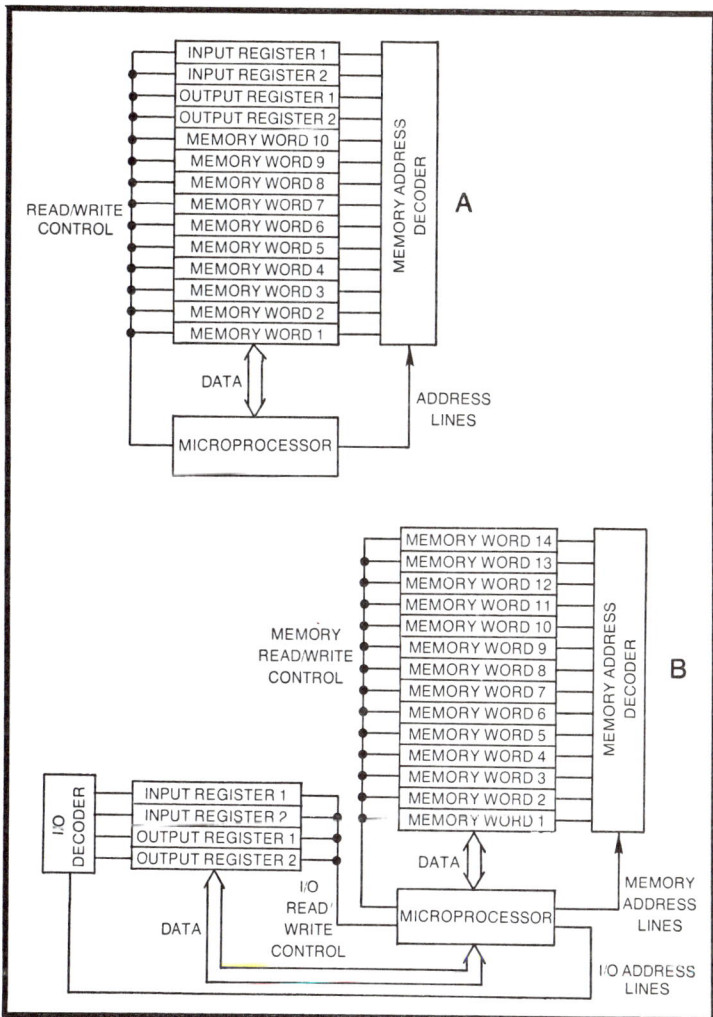

Fig. 7-6. Two methods of addressing an I/O device. At A the I/O device is shown as a memory location. The total memory locations are reduced from 14 to 10, but the control circuits are simpler. At B the memory and I/O addressing are separate and more complex. However, four extra memory locations are gained.

INTERRUPTS

Often I/O devices are extremely slow when compared to microprocessor speed. For example, a good typist at a teleprinter keyboard can generate a new character once every 10th of a second. In the course of one-tenth of a second, most microprocessors can execute 10,000 to 50,000 instructions. For this reason, it is a waste of time for the microprocessor to be tied up waiting for a character to be generated at the teleprinter keyboard when it can be doing other things in the meantime.

Two methods of servicing I/O devices are used. If the microprocessor is not required to perform any additional function while waiting for the I/O device, a *polling routine* is used. A polling routine regularly tests the I/O status word until the external device is ready. Once the polling routine indicates the I/O device is ready, the device is serviced. After the device is serviced, the microprocessor either processes the information or returns to the polling routine, depending upon the program.

If the programmer wishes to make use of the microprocessor when it is not servicing an I/O device, an interrupt is used. Using the interrupt technique, the microprocessor works on a designated problem until the I/O device is ready. When the I/O device is ready, it interrupts the microprocessor by signaling a special microprocessor input line. When the microprocessor receives an interrupt signal, it stops processing the present program at the completion of the current instruction cycle. The current value of the program counter is stored. A new value is placed in the program counter, starting the microprocessor on a subroutine to service the interrupting I/O device. Once the I/O service routine is complete, the microprocessor continues the main program.

A single-level interrupt services one device. If there are a number of external devices connected to the interrupt line, the initial part of the service routine must poll each of the possible interrupting devices to determine which one caused the interrupt. If this technique is not fast enough, multiple priority interrupts are used. With a multiple priority interrupt scheme, each I/O or interrupting device is assigned a priority. Each I/O or interrupting device is also assigned a specific memory address where its service routine is stored.

For example, the number-three device interrupts the microprocessor requesting service. The microprocessor completes the current instruction of the program in process and stores the value of the program counter. It then begins to service the number-three device with the routine stored at the number-three interrupt vector. During the process of servicing the number-three device, the number-two device generates an interrupt. The microprocessor stops servicing the number-three device and begins a service routine for the number-two device. Once the routine for the number-two device is complete, the microprocessor completes the service routine for the number-three device. It then returns to the main program. *Multiple level interrupts* are often four to eight levels deep. Usually, the highest priority interrupts are assigned to power failure and power up routines, with communications I/O devices assuming a somewhat lower priority.

Chapter 8

Input/Output Devices

This chapter briefly reviews some of the various forms of I/O devices used to communicate with microprocessors. One of the most common I/O devices is the teletypewriter. The teletypewriter is simply a fancy electric typewriter. Another form of I/O device uses the keyboard with a television-like display. A third form of communication uses a switch register. Each of these common microprocessor I/O devices is discussed, including its advantages and disadvantages.

SWITCH REGISTERS

The most basic microprocessor input device is the *switch register*. The switch register is simply a row of switches; each switch corresponds to a single bit in the microprocessor data word. When the user desires to enter information into the microprocessor, the switches are set up for a logic 1 and down for a logic 0. These switches represent the bit pattern for the desired input word. As the *deposit switch* is depressed, this data word is placed in a previously addressed memory location.

Memory addressing is also done with the switch register. Therefore, a switch register for an 8-bit microprocessor may well contain 16 switches, as 16 bits are required to address a memory location. Only eight of these switches are used when data is being entered. Figure 8-1 shows a hypothetical switch register. Beside the 16 address/data switches, 2 additional switches are shown. Actuating the *load address switch* causes the microprocessor to examine all 16 switches in the switch register. The binary number read from the 16 switches is used to address the microprocessor memory word.

Once the address is loaded, a second binary word is entered into the lower eight bits of the switch register, again setting the switches up for a logic 1 and down for a logic 0. When the deposit switch is actuated, the binary word represented by these eight bits of the switch register is loaded into the addressed memory word.

Other switches may accompany the load address and deposit switches. Common switches are: a *start* (or *go*) switch, which begins program execution; a *halt switch* which terminates program execution; a *single cycle switch* which only allows a microprocessor to execute one instruction at a time; and a *continue switch* which lets the program continue executing from the point where it was halted. Sometimes an *examine switch* may be found on microprocessor system panels. The examine switch allows the user to view the contents of sequential memory locations each time the switch is depressed. The examine switch is particularly useful for examining memory contents to determine if a program has been loaded properly.

BINARY PANEL DISPLAY

The simplest microprocessor output display is a binary lamp register. Like the switch register, there are 16 lamps for an 8-bit microprocessor. All 16 lamps are used when viewing memory address information, each lamp representing 1 bit of memory address. When the lamp is on, it represents a logic 1. When the lamp is off, it represents a logic 0. When lamps are displaying data in a register or memory location, only 8 of the 16 lamps are used. Sometimes lamps in the corresponding

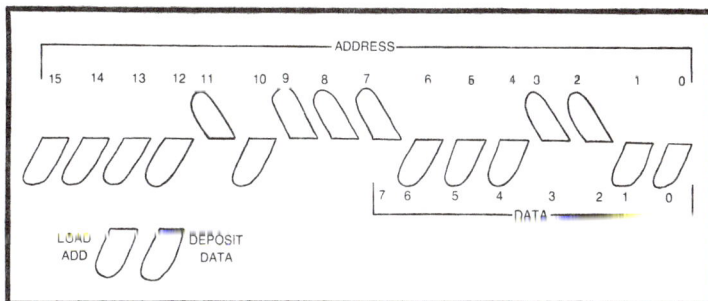

Fig. 8-1. A simple 16-bit switch register. All 16 data switches are used to input an address. The low-order eight (0-7) are used to input data. The LOAD ADDRESS and DEPOSIT DATA switches place the switch register in the proper microprocessor locations.

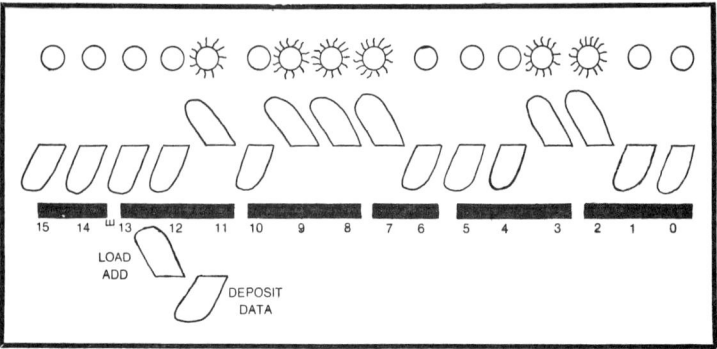

Fig. 8-2. A binary display added to the switch register of Fig. 8-1. Note the LOAD ADDress switch is raised and the binary lamps are indicating the switch pattern. Also note colored grouping bars added under the switches for ease of converting the LO byte (switches 0-7) and the HI byte (switches 8 – 15) to octal.

switches are grouped with coloring or physical placement into threes or fours. This grouping facilitates mental translation of the binary numbers into either octal or hexidecimal notation. Most microprocessors use *light emitting diode (LED)* displays. Figure 8-2 shows such a binary display attached to the switch register of Fig. 8-1.

OCTAL AND HEXIDECIMAL FRONT PANELS

A few systems no longer make use of individual bit lights and switches. These systems use 7-segment LED displays such as those found on digital clocks. These displays show the address and data information as octal or hexidecimal numbers. The use of 7-segment LED displays eliminates the need for the programmer to convert from the common octal or hexidecimal notation into binary. Usually the octal or hexidecimal display is accompanied by an octal or hexidecimal keyboard, much like a calculator keyboard. This keyboard eliminates the need for individual bit switches as described in the switch register discussion. In these situations, the 16-bit switch register is replaced by an 8- or 16-key *switchpad*. Figure 8-3 shows a simplified example of an octal system.

THE TELEPRINTER

One of the most common alphanumeric input/output communications devices for microcomputers and microprocessors is the *teleprinter*. The teleprinter is essentially an electric typewriter with communications

114

capability. The teletypewriter keyboard generates signals in serial form. At the microprocessor, these serial signals are converted into parallel words for processing. Parallel words in the microprocessor are converted into serial signals. The serial signals are sent to the teleprinter and are typed out.

One of the most common teleprinter terminals is the Teletype Corporation Model 33. Fig. 8-4 is a picture of a Teletype Model 33ASR (Automatic Send/Receive). The Model 33ASR sends and receives at a rate of 10 characters per second (110 baud). Commonly, the Model 33 communicates over 2 pairs of wires, using a 20 mA serial current loop. The popularity of the Teletype stems basically from its low cost. The cost of a Model 33ASR is in the neighborhood of $1,000. Although this may seem very high to the hobbyist, it is indeed one of the lowest cost, hard copy (printing) terminals available. The hard copy output of a Teletype usually comes in the form of a long roll of paper 8 1/2-inches wide. The Model 33 prints 72 columns across the page before a new line is required.

VIDEO TERMINALS

The *video terminal* is becoming quite popular. Video terminals are faster, quieter, and are becoming lower cost

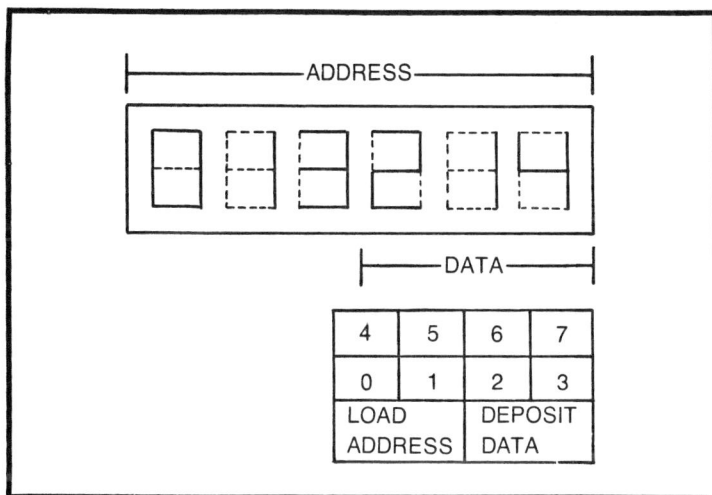

Fig. 8-3. An octal keypad/display. Note the binary input and output is eliminated; all entries and readings are in octal. The octal display reads the same number as the binary display of Fig. 8-2. Note the highest octal number which can be displayed is 377 377. This is equivalent to binary:

11111111   11111111.

Fig. 8-4. The Teletype Corporation Model 33 ASR Teleprinter. One of the most common hard copy I/O devices. The 33 ASR also includes provisions to read and punch 8-level paper tape. Photograph courtesy Teletype Corporation.

than many printing terminals. The cost of most video terminals lies between $1,500 and $2,000, although terminal prices are rapidly decreasing. Teleprinters tend to be slow, operating at speeds of 10, 15, or 30 characters per second. Video terminals operate up to speeds of 960 characters per second (9600 baud). These higher speeds are especially useful when scanning large quantities of data. Frequently, there is no requirement for hard copy. The video terminal is often useful when the microprocessor is used to play games, view long programs, or review information. A typical video terminal is shown in Fig. 8-5.

The video terminal keyboard is similar to the teleprinter keyboard, except video terminals usually offer both upper- and lowercase letters, whereas teleprinters are often restricted to uppercase only. Characters are displayed on the video terminal in an 80 column by 12-, 20-, or 24-row format. Needless to say, the more sophisticated (and expensive) the terminal the greater the number of characters displayed.

Many video terminals offer special features called up by typing special *command keys*. One of these special features is *scroll*. When the video terminal is in the scroll mode, the first line disappears after the last line is filled up, the lines moved up to fill in the gap, and a new line is typed in the last empty space.

When the video terminal is not in the scroll mode, the data typed on additional lines after the screen is filled is lost. Most video terminals features a *cursor*. The cursor is a small underscore, which may be blinking or not blinking. It shows

Fig. 8-5. The Digital Equipment Corporation Model VT-52 video terminal. This KSR (Keyboard Send/Receive) terminal operates at speeds up to 9600 baud, uses upper and lower case characters and has an 80 column by 24 line display. Photograph courtesy of Digital Equipment Corporation.

where the next character will be typed. These terminals usually have cursor control. Cursor control permits the cursor to be sent *home* (the upper left hand corner of the screen), sent to the beginning of a line, moved to the right, moved to the left, moved up, or moved down. Many video terminals have other special features which depend upon the desired purpose of the terminal. For example, a video terminal and a microprocessor may be used to replace a cash register. This video terminal has numerous special keys and characters to enable it to perform the cash register function.

LINE PRINTERS

Because the video terminal is unable to give hard copy, the user is often forced to connect a printer to the microprocessor. The printer is called upon when hard copy is necessary. Other communications take place using the video terminal. Often the hardware to do this job is called a *line printer*. A line printer differs from a teletypewriter in that it prints information one line at a time. A teletypewriter prints one character at a time. Line printers are designed to print large volumes of data very rapidly. They are usually expensive devices and not customarily found on the small microprocessor systems. Printing speeds of most line printers are given in lines per minute rather than in characters per second.

MODEMS

Modem is a contraction of the words *m*odulator and *dem*odulator. The modem is a device used to conduct serial transmissions from remote devices, such as video terminals and teleprinters, to a microprocessor. The *modulator* portion of the modem converts the serial keyboard signals into high and low frequency *tones*. These tones are transmitted over ordinary *telephone lines* in the same manner as voice signals are transmitted. At the other end of the telephone line a modem *demodulator* converts these variable tones into serial signals to communicate information to the waiting microprocessor. A block diagram showing two modems and a telephone line connecting a remote teleprinter to a microprocessor system is shown in Fig. 8-6. Different *tone pairs* are used by the *answer modem* and the *transmit modem*. Therefore, the microprocessor may send information to the teleprinter while the teleprinter is sending the microprocessor information. *Bidirectional communication* occurs over a single telephone line.

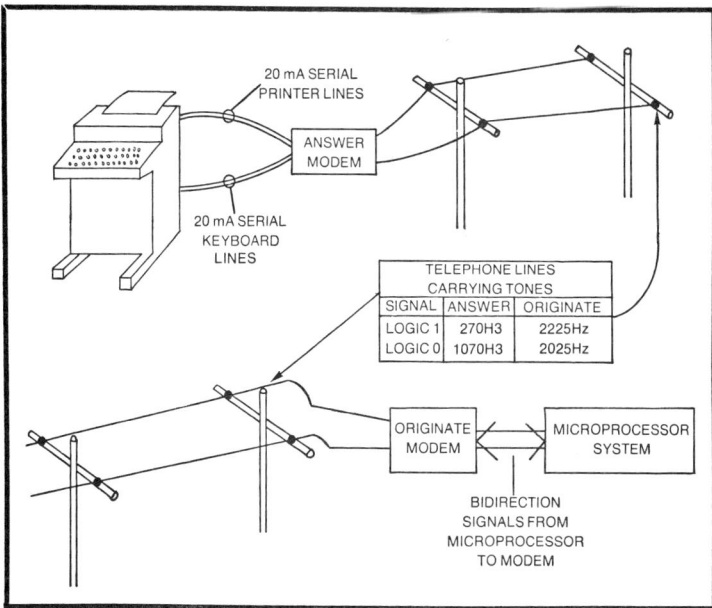

Fig. 8-6. A teleprinter communicating with a microprocessor via telephone lines. The serial logic 1s and 0s are converted to tones by the modems which convert these signals back to data words at the other end.

MASS STORAGE AS AN I/O DEVICE

Often the total amount of memory required to store all the programs used by a microprocessor or all the data generated by a microprocessor exceeds the total memory the microprocessor can address and/or the total amount of main memory that can be economically attached to the microprocessor. When the storage requirements exceed main memory capability, *mass storage* is utilized. The common storage media is either paper or magnetic materials. One of the more well known forms of paper storage is the *IBM card*. The IBM card was used for many years by the computer industry but has not found its way into the microprocessor industry to any great extent. This is primarily because of the expense involved in reading cards.

PUNCHED PAPER TAPE

Figure 8-7 shows a length of 8-level *punched paper tape*. Paper tape serves as an inexpensive, nonvolatile mass storage directly compatible with many teleprinters. The Teletype Model 33ASR accomplishes the automatic send-receive function with the 8-level punched paper tape. The Model 33ASR

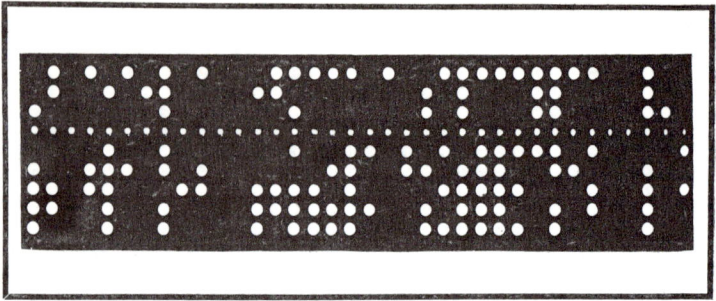

Fig. 8-7. Eight level 1-inch punched paper tape. The row of small holes fits a sprocket which moves the tape. Binary information is contained in the eight larger holes. Each row contains one 8-bit word.

is capable of reading 8-level tape at a speed of 10 characters per second. It is also capable of punching 8-level paper tape at 10 characters per second.

Again referring to Fig. 8-7, note that up to eight holes may be punched in the paper tape. A hole represents a logic 1, and the absence of a hole represents a logic 0. The paper tape punch punches the appropriate holes in response to information from the microprocessor. Later the paper tape may be placed in a *paper tape reader* which reads this information and sends each byte to the microprocessor to be loaded in memory. Paper tape is quite common. The Model 33ASR Teletype includes a paper tape reader/punch for just a few additional dollars. Although these are noisy and moderately slow, the paper tape reader/punch provides a convenient, low cost mass storage for program and data information. Once the user has the luxury of storing a program on punched paper tape, the latter loading the microprocessor memory at 10 characters per second, the thought of hand entry of this information via the switch register disappears. The Model 33ASR is not the only way to read and punch paper tape. Individual high speed paper tape readers (1000 characters per second) and punches are available. However, these are not inexpensive.

MAGNETIC TAPE

As noted earlier, many of the microprocessor hobby applications use simplified video terminals, called *TV typewriters*. The TV typewriter, of course, does not contain a paper tape reader/punch. Nonetheless, the hobbyist also wishes to store program information. This need created a search for a low-cost mass storage medium. The medium chosen was the standard Phillips Cassette. *Cassette recorders* are low-cost (usually in the $30 to $50 range) and the cassettes themselves are quite inexpensive. The technique for recording and playback converts the binary information into two tones, one for a logic 1 and another for a logic 0. The tones are recorded at a rate of about 30 characters (bytes) per second.

At this rate, the cassette is three times faster than the 10 character per second paper tape reader/punch. The recording format is called the *Kansas City Standard*. The exact technical details of the Kansas City Standard are covered in a number of computer hobbyist magazines and books. Although it is nowhere near as reliable as punched paper tape or other more professional magnetic recording media, it is definitely a very low cost way to record digital information from your microprocessor. Information, of course, may also be transmitted to the microprocessor by playing back this tape. Once again, the tones from the tape are converted into logic signals. The logic signals are then applied to the microprocessor I/O channel.

THE FLOPPY DISC

On the more advanced hobbyist microprocessor-based systems, neither paper tape nor the cassette provides an adequate volume or speed for storing digital information. The next step is to move to a spinning magnetic disc, much like a 45 rpm phonograph record. This is called a *floppy disc*. The floppy disc actually consists of an 8-inch diameter donut made of magnetic recording tape. Although this donut is eight inches in diameter, it is only a few thousandths of an inch thick. The donut is sealed inside a lightweight cardboard envelope. The envelope has an oblong slot in one side permitting the record/playback head to be placed against the magnetic material. The physical characteristics of a floppy disc are shown in Fig. 8-8. Figure 8-9 shows floppy disc sectoring. Instead of operating on a spiral groove, as the phonograph operates, the floppy disc has 77 concentric tracks. Each track is divided into 26 or 32 sectors. The difference between 26 and 32 sectors is a matter of IBM or non-IBM format. Each sector contains 128 bytes. Therefore, the entire floppy disc can contain 256,256 bytes of data with the 26 sector format or 315,392 bytes of data with the 32 sector format.

As noted earlier, the floppy disc is choosen for both speed and recording density. The disc spins at 360 rpm. In other words, the disc requires 166 ms for one revolution. This means the average time to access information on a track is approximately half that time or 83 ms. Obviously, this is much faster than the cassettes or paper tape. For example, it may take 30 minutes to search one side of a C60 cassette, whereas all 77 tracks of a floppy disc can be searched completely in 12.8 seconds.

Obviously, one does not get something for nothing. Floppy discs are not as inexpensive as either paper tape or cassettes. $1,000 to $2,000 is required for a single floppy disc system. A normal system utilizes two floppy discs and is a $2,000-plus system.

The floppy disc system breaks into three major areas. First is a mechanical package or the drive. The drive spins the floppy disc, advances the head across the 77 tracks, signals the electronics package when the sector hole passes and keeps the record/playback signals to high level signals which can be processed by digital logic. The drive electronics package may also contain some additional signal processing electronics which convert the serial bit stream from the playback head to a parallel word. Third is the disc controller. The disc controller handles the data manipulation functions for the microprocessor. When the microprocessor asks the floppy disc to retrieve a particular information file located on a particular track and sector, the controller sends signals to the drive electronics to start the motors, advance the head to the appropriate track, and record all information on that track. The approriate sector information is then sent to the

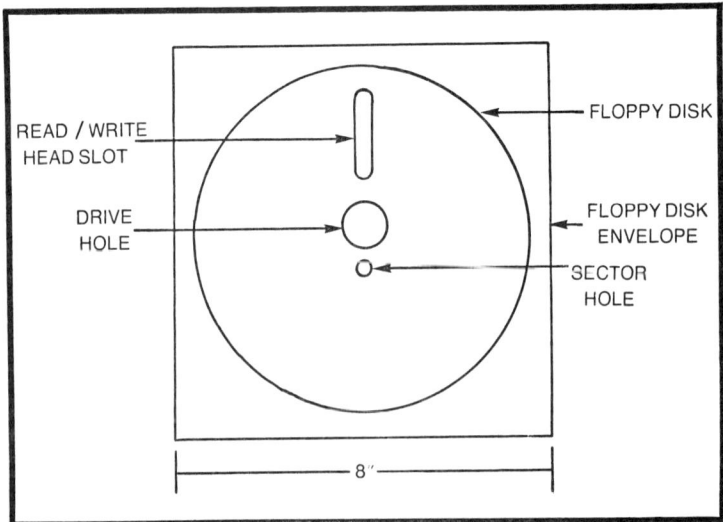

Fig. 8-8. The floppy disc in its jacket. The jacket has openings for the drive, number one sector identification, and the read/write head.

122

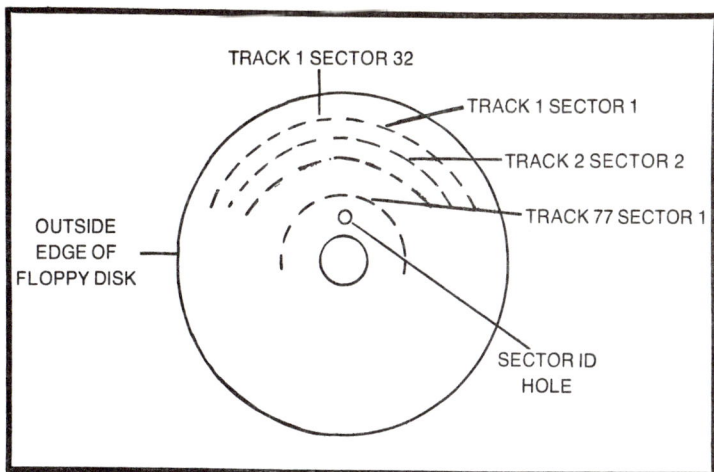

Fig. 8-9. The floppy disc recording format. Each disc can have up to 77 tracks. Each track is divided into 26 or 32 sectors. The number one sector is identified by the sector hole punched in the floppy.

microprocessor memory, usually using Direct Memory Access (DMA). Normally, the controller electronics is capable of handling a number of floppy disc drives.

Floppy disc prices are dropping rapidly. Dual floppy systems will soon be available to the microprocessor hobbyist for less than $1,000.

123

Chapter 9

The Microprocessor Instruction Set

The microprocessor fetches instructions from memory, interprets or decodes them, and then executes the particular function required. If the microprocessor is capable of 56 different operations, there must be 56 different instruction words. When fetched, each instruction word is interpreted differently than any of the other 55 instruction words. The list of instruction words and the functions they perform is called the microprocessor *instruction set*.

ARCHITECTURE

The instruction set for each microprocessor is different from any other microprocessor. Instruction sets differ in two ways. First, the instruction words used by the processor to carry out identical functions are different. For example, the Intel 8080 uses the binary word 001111100 to increment the accumulator. Their 6800 uses the binary word 01001100 to increment the accumulator. Second, the internal organization of each microprocessor is different. This is frequently termed its *architecture*. This difference requires different instructions. For example, the 8080 has one accumulator and four working registers. The 6800 has two full accumulators and no working registers.

For most microprocessors the instruction is contained in one byte. However, some instructions refer to one or two additional bytes of data. These additional bytes may be used as data for the instruction. They also can be used as address values for the memory address register or the the program counter. When the instruction refers to additional bytes of data, these bytes follow the instruction directly in the program sequence. Such instructions are referred to as *multiple byte instructions*. Multiple byte instructions may be two or three bytes long.

The first word of any instruction, single or multiple byte, is called an *op code*, the abbreviation for operation code. The op code is interpreted by the control logic. If the op code indicates there are additional bytes following the op code byte, these additional bytes, called *operands*, are fetched as the instruction is executed.

In this chapter we examine many of the common microprocessor instructions. Simple microprocessor registers are used to demonstrate the effects of the instruction. When working with a particular microprocessor, one of the best ways to understand the various instructions is to exercise each instruction. The best way to do this is with a microprocessor trainer or breadboard. However, if this is not possible, the technique in this chapter is useful to become familiar with the microprocessor's instruction set.

In this chapter, instructions are categorized as best possible. They are covered in the order of data transfer instructions, arithmetic and logical instructions, subroutine instructions, and special processor instructions. It is impossible to make completely clean-cut categories for the various instructions. Therefore, there may be some instructions which appear under one heading which could conceivably be in another.

DATA TRANSFER INSTRUCTIONS

Data transfer instructions shift data between specified registers, or between a specified register and a memory location. The memory location used is pointed to (addressed) by the memory address register. The instruction contains binary identification for each of the registers involved. The binary identification for the memory address register is different when it is the data source itself or if it points to the destination of the data in memory.

For example, the 8080 microprocessor uses the form 01DDDSSS. The 01 indicates a data transfer instruction. The DDD is the destination register identification. The SSS is the source register identification. If data is being transferred to or from memory, the memory address register is used as a pointer. In this case, the SSS or the DDD is replaced by 110. The 110 indicates the memory address register is the *pointer*, not the source or the destination.

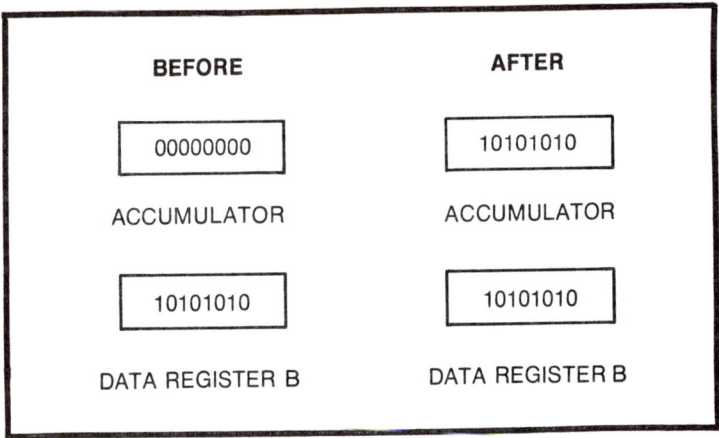

Fig. 9-1. A register data transfer. Data is transferred from data register B to the accumulator. The destination or source could have been any register or a memory location. Note the original value in data register B is not destroyed.

Figure 9-1 shows a register transfer instruction. The binary word 10101010 is transferred from register B to the accumulator. After the transfer, *both* register B and the accumulator contain the value 10101010.

Occasionally the programmer wishes to load a register or a memory location with a predetermined value. For this situation the two-byte TRANSFER IMMEDIATE instruction is used. The first byte of the transfer immediate instruction tells the processor the second word of the instruction is to be treated as data to be placed in the indicated register.

If a two-byte register, such as the program counter or the memory address register is to be loaded in the immediate mode, a three-byte instruction is used. In these cases the second and third byte of the instruction are used as data values for the desired register.

A transfer immediate instruction is shown in Fig. 9-2. A memory diagram is shown at the top of the figure. The data transfer immediate instruction (01111011) is followed by the data value 10101010 to be transferred into data register C. Below the memory diagram, before and after versions of data register C are shown. Data transfer instructions are called MOVE instructions in some microprocessor instruction sets.

ARITHMETIC AND LOGICAL INSTRUCTIONS

Arithmetic and logical instructions are used to process data in a register or memory location. An arithmetic or logical instruction arithmetically or logically combines the data in the source with data present in the destination. The ADD instruction is an example of an arithmetic operation.

In order to be combined with the present data in an arithmetic or logical manner, data must pass through the *Arithmetic and Logic Unit* (ALU). This requirement eliminates certain registers and sometimes eliminates memory from being the destination. The registers (and memory) involved are a function of the particular microprocessor.

The source for data for an arithmetic or logical instruction may be any of the CPU registers or memory. Again the sources available for these instructions depend on the microprocessor in use.

The basic arithmetic instruction is binary addition. Figure 9-3 demonstrates a binary addition from data register B into the accumulator. This is the ADD instruction. Most microprocessors offer a second version of the ADD instruction

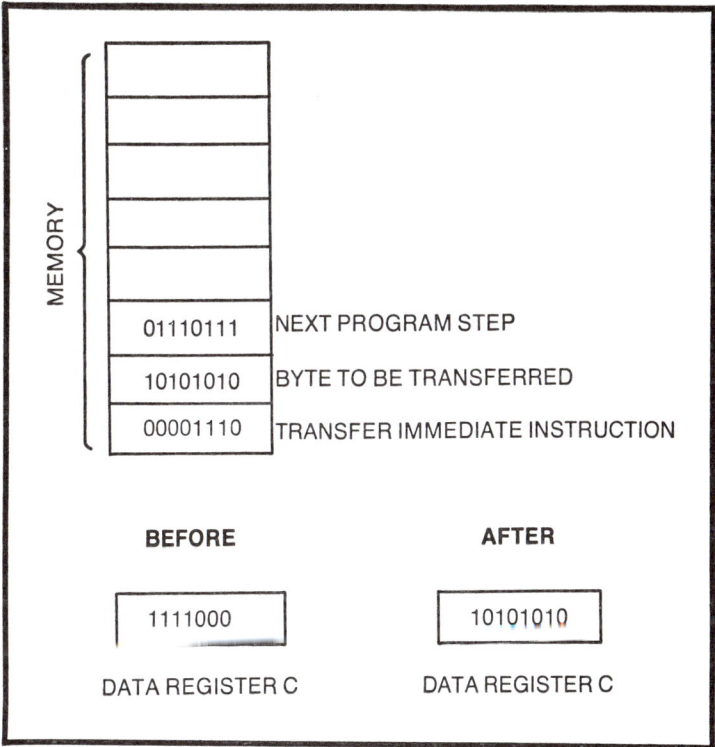

Fig. 9-2. A data TRANSFER IMMEDIATE. The second byte of the data transfer instruction (01111011) is placed in data register C replacing the original 1111000 with the 10101010 of the second byte.

127

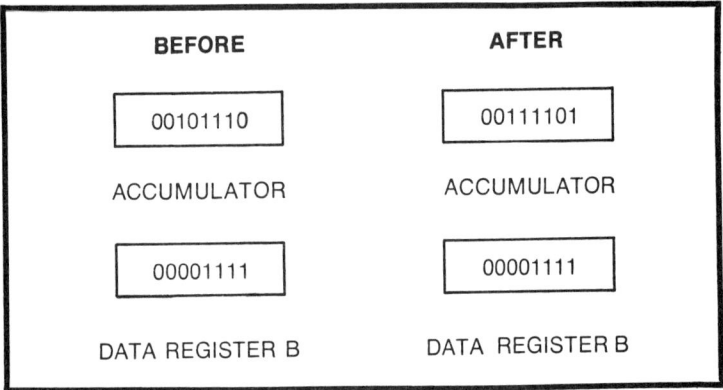

	BEFORE	AFTER
	00101110	00111101
	ACCUMULATOR	ACCUMULATOR
	00001111	00001111
	DATA REGISTER B	DATA REGISTER B

Fig. 9-3. Binary addition of the contents of data register B with the accumulator. After the addition the accumulator contains the result. Data register B retains its original value. This arithmetic operation did not result in a carry.

called ADD WITH CARRY. This means the addition is performed using the carry (if any) generated from a previous addition. For a complete explanation of binary addition see Chapter 3. Figure 9-4 is a repeat of the binary addition of Fig. 9-3. but a carry from the status register has been added.

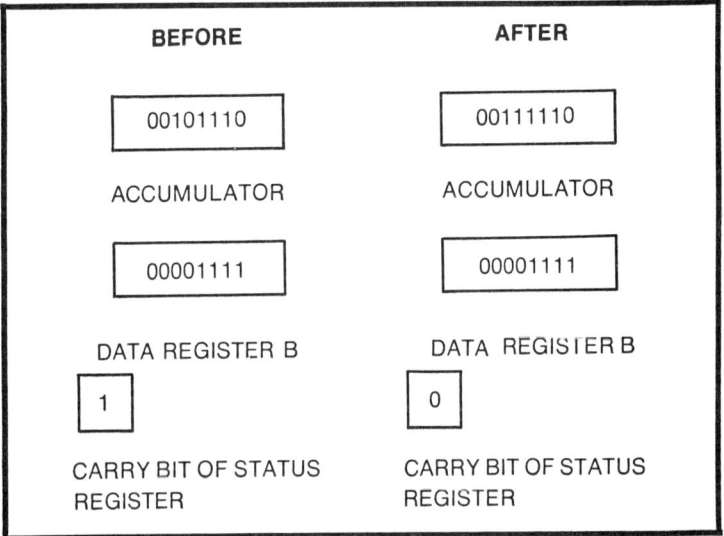

	BEFORE	AFTER
	00101110	00111110
	ACCUMULATOR	ACCUMULATOR
	00001111	00001111
	DATA REGISTER B	DATA REGISTER B
	1	0
	CARRY BIT OF STATUS REGISTER	CARRY BIT OF STATUS REGISTER

Fig. 9-4. Binary addition using the carry. Note the carry bit of the status register is a 1 before the addition from a previous addition. After this addition the carry bit of the status register is set to zero as the addition produces no carry.

The programmer may use two methods to perform binary subtraction. Most microprocessors have a SUBTRACT instruction. The SUBTRACT instruction automatically performs all the functions done by a software subtraction routine. As with the ADD instruction there is usually a SUBTRACT WITH BORROW instruction. If there is no SUBTRACT instruction available, a software routine program called *two's complement* is used. Again see Chapter 3 for a detailed explanation.

Microprocessor arithmetic is binary in nature. Unfortunately most of the work done by humans is decimal in nature. The conversion between decimal and binary is normally handled by short programs dedicated to this function. Some microprocessors offer a special arithmetic instruction called DECIMAL ADJUST. If two Binary Coded Decimal (BCD) numbers are operated on by an ADD instruction, the result is neither binary nor BCD. The *decimal adjust* instruction converts the binary addition of two BCD numbers into a BCD result. Figure 9-6 shows the result of a DECIMAL ADJUST instruction. Unfortunately, most

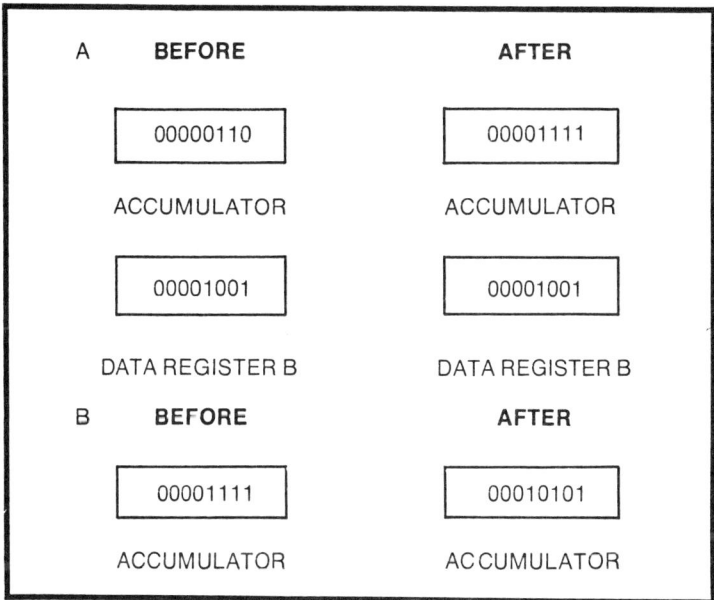

Fig. 9-5. At A, two BCD numbers (6=00000110 in the accumulator and 9=00001001 in data register B) are operated on by a binary ADD. Afterwards the accumulator contains the result (15=00001111). At B, the accumulator is shown before and after the DECIMAL ADJUST instruction (0001=1 and 0101=5)

BEFORE	AFTER
11110000	11110101
ACCUMULATOR	ACCUMULATOR
10101010	10101010
MEMORY	MEMORY

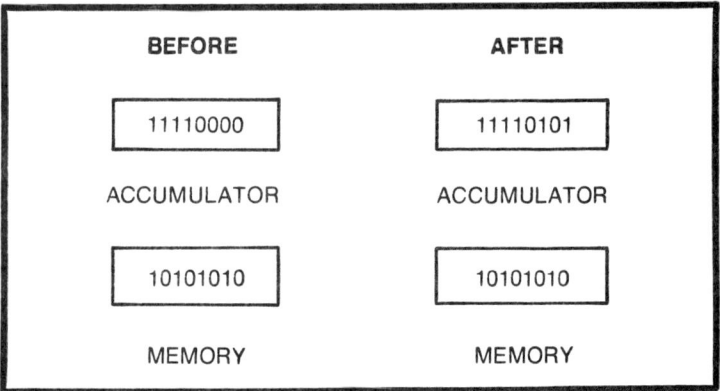

Fig. 9-6. The OR instruction. Each bit of the source—in this example, the contents of a memory location—is logically ORed with the contents of the accumulator. The results are left in the accumulator.

microprocessors do not include instructions to convert BCD to binary or binary to BCD. These operations must be performed in software by the programmer.

The arithmetic instructions also include a group of IMMEDIATE instructions. The ADD IMMEDIATE instruction adds the second byte of the instruction to the indicated destination. If the microprocessor includes a SUBTRACT instruction, there is SUBTRACT IMMEDIATE instruction as well. ADD IMMEDIATE and SUBTRACT IMMEDIATE instructions also have ADD IMMEDIATE WITH CARRY and

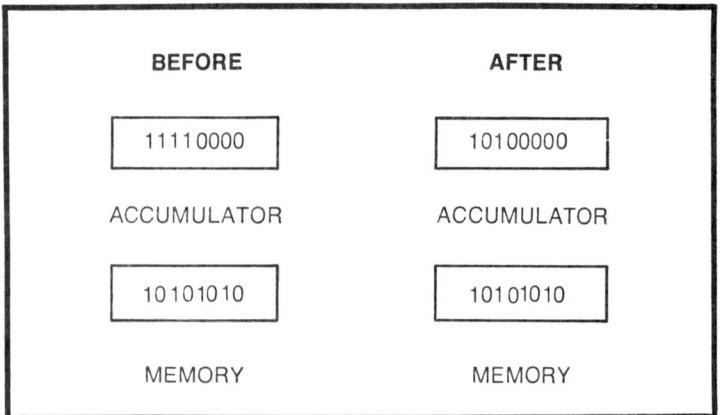

BEFORE	AFTER
11110000	10100000
ACCUMULATOR	ACCUMULATOR
10101010	10101010
MEMORY	MEMORY

Fig. 9-7. The AND instruction. Each bit contained in the memory location (source) is logically ANDed with the data in the accumulator. Compare the results of an OR instruction in Fig. 9-6 with the AND instruction here.

BEFORE	AFTER
11110000	01011010
ACCUMULATOR	ACCUMULATOR
10101010	10101010
MEMORY	MEMORY

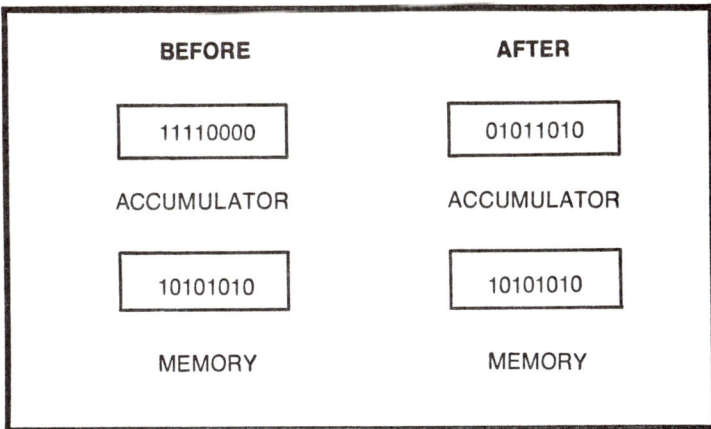

Fig. 9-8. The EXCLUSIVE OR instruction.

SUBTRACT IMMEDIATE WITH BORROW instructions to complete the list.

The *logical instructions* include a fairly large number of standard operations for all microprocessors as well as some instructions unique to a few microprocessors. The logical operations AND, OR, and EXCLUSIVE OR are common to most instruction sets. Figures 9-6 through 9-9 give examples of the OR, AND and EXCLUSIVE OR instructions.

Registers and memory locations can normally be *incremented* or *decremented* by use of a logical instruction. When a register is incremented, binary value is increased by one. Decrementing a register reduces the value by one. The effects of incrementing and decrementing are the same as

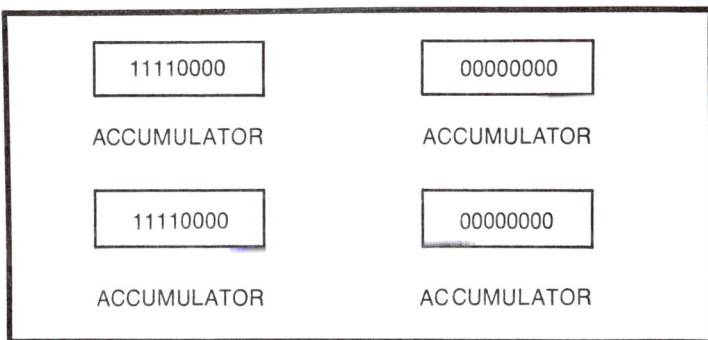

11110000	00000000
ACCUMULATOR	ACCUMULATOR
11110000	00000000
ACCUMULATOR	ACCUMULATOR

Fig. 9-9. The EXCLUSIVE OR instruction used as a CLEAR ACCUMULATOR. The accumulator is EXCLUSIVE ORed with itself. The result is all zeros.

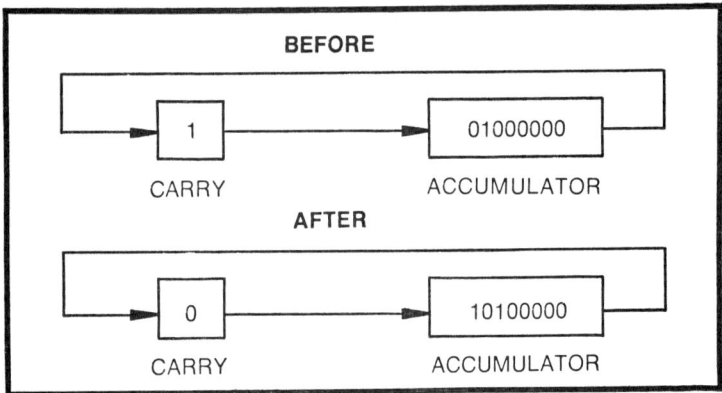

Fig. 9-10. ROTATE RIGHT. The least significant bit of the accumulator is passed to the carry bit. The carry bit is passed to the most significant bit of the accumulator.

adding one to or subtracting one from the register. The INCREMENT and DECREMENT instructions simply require one less instruction to do the job.

The logical instructions include both the SHIFT and the ROTATE instructions. Both the shift and the rotate instructions use the carry status register bit. Shift instructions (SHIFT RIGHT and SHIFT LEFT) enter a zero from the starting end of the shift and the last bit is lost. Rotate instructions circulate data through the carry bit and back to the starting point. The definitions of *shift* and *rotate* are not

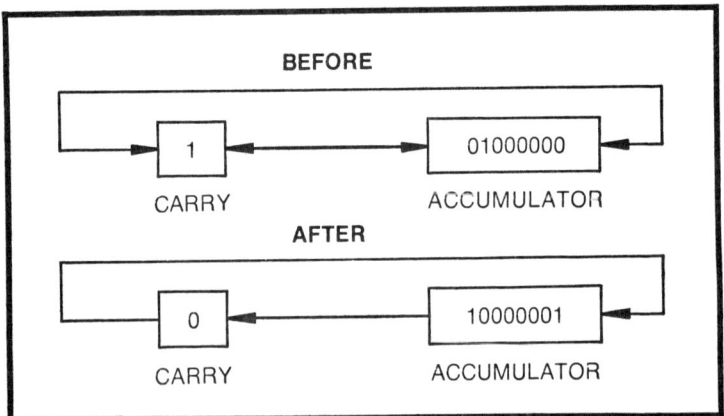

Fig. 9-11 ROTATE LEFT. The most significant bit of the accumulator is passed to the carry bit. The carry bit is passed to the least significant bit of the accumulator.

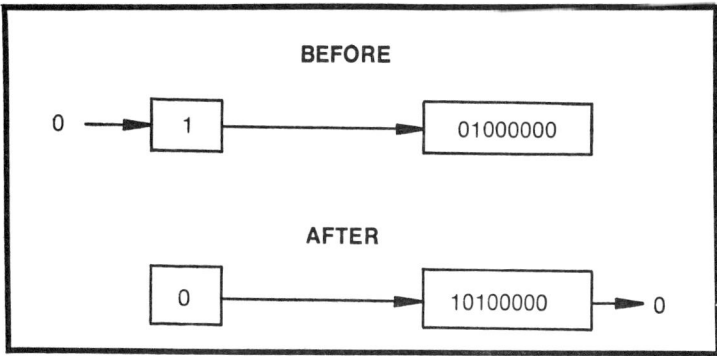

Fig. 9-12. Shift right. The least significant bit of the accumulator is lost. The carry is passed to the most significant accumulator bit, and a zero is placed in the carry bit.

used with a great deal of uniformity. The user must take extra care to thoroughly understand the manufacturer's explanations of shift and rotate for the particular microprocessor. Figures 9-10 through 9-13 show examples of shift and rotate.

The *complement instruction* changes all ones in a register to zeros and all zeros to ones. A two's complement subtracts the contents of the register from zero and places that answer in the register. Complement instructions are not found universally on all microprocessor instruction sets. Figure 9-14 shows examples of accumulator complementing instructions.

The COMPARE instruction if a full (four, eight, etc,. bit) EXCLUSIVE OR between the source and the destination. The

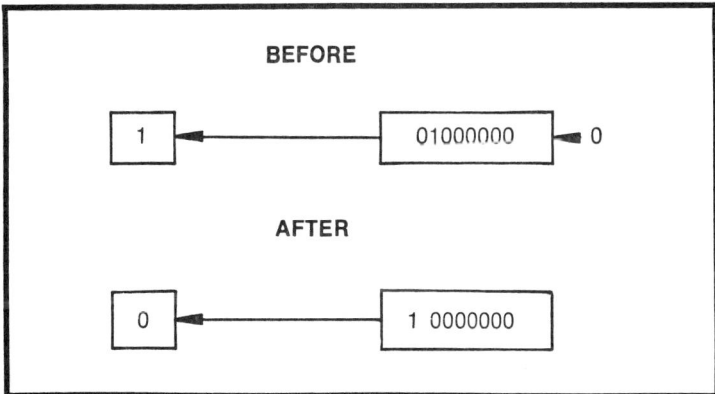

Fig. 9-13. Shift left. The least significant accumulator bit is replaced by a zero. The carry is replaced by the most significant accumulator bit and the original carry bit is lost.

133

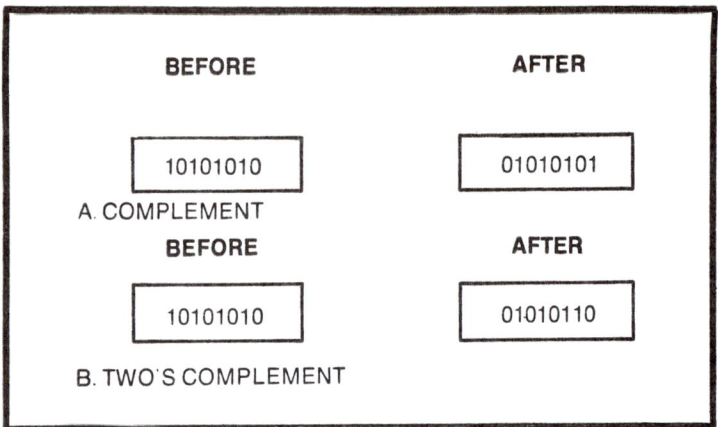

BEFORE	AFTER

A. COMPLEMENT

B. TWO'S COMPLEMENT

Fig. 9-14. The COMPLEMENT instruction is shown at A. All ones are changed to zeroes and all zeroes are changed to ones. At B, the two's complement instruction is shown. This instruction permits easy binary subtraction without first checking to determine the sign of the larger number.

status-register bits are set by the COMPARE instruction, but the registers which are compared are not disturbed. COMPARE instructions are used to test a register for a certain bit pattern. Their advantage is in not having to replace the contents of the register after testing. This is the case, for example, if the AND instruction is used as a test.

JUMP (BRANCH) INSTRUCTIONS

The effect of the JUMP instruction is to change the contents of the program counter. The terms *jump* and *branch* are used interchangeably. The simplest jump instruction is the JUMP UNCONDITIONAL. As the name implies, the instruction directs the program counter to be loaded with a new value. This instruction is executed independently of any other conditions within the microprocessor. The new program-counter value is contained in the program itself. Jump instructions are three-byte immediate instructions. The first byte is the jump instruction. The second and third bytes contain the new program counter value. Of course this implies the programmer knows where he is jumping to. Figure 9-15 shows the effect of a jump instruction on the program counter. Note that the HI and LO bytes of the program counter are drawn from successive points in memory.

The CONDITIONAL JUMP test specifies bits of the status register. The new program counter value is only placed in the program counter if the status register conditions are met. There is a different CONDITIONAL JUMP instruction to test each of the status bits. With five status bits, there are five conditional jump tests possible. The total number of conditional jump instructions may well double as most microprocessors have instructions to test each bit of the status register for true (a logic 1) or false (a logic 0).

Any time a jump instruction is executed the current contents of the program counter are lost. Again the programmer must be very careful when he reads the manufacturer's literature. Some refer to subroutine instructions as jump instructions. JUMP TO SUBROUTINE

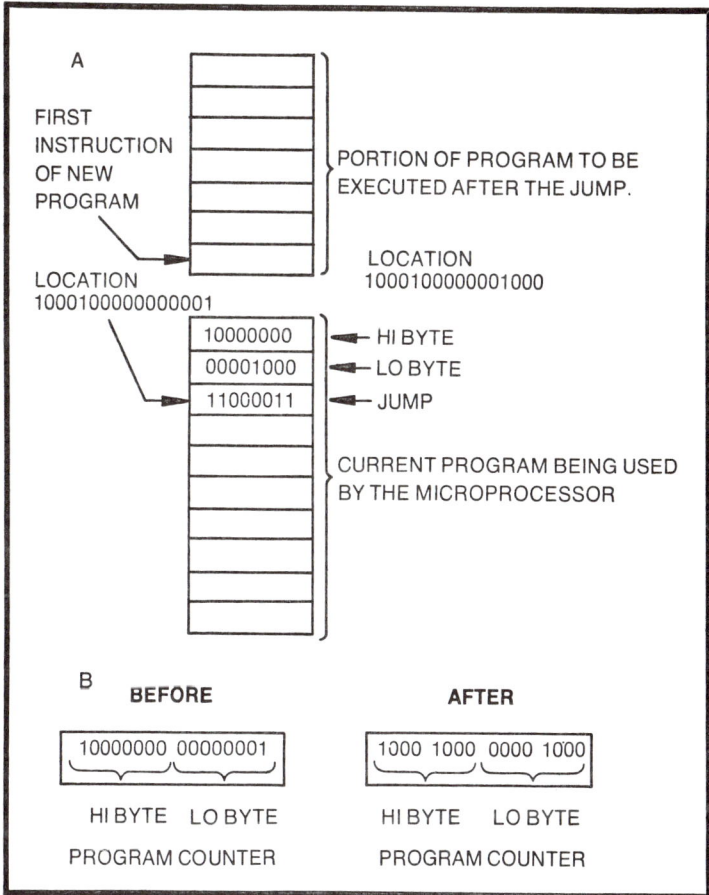

Fig. 9-15. At A, a memory diagram shows the locations of a JUMP instruction, the two IMMEDIATE address bytes, and the program at this new location. At B, the program counter for A is shown. Note that both the HI byte and the LO byte are changed after execution of the JUMP instruction.

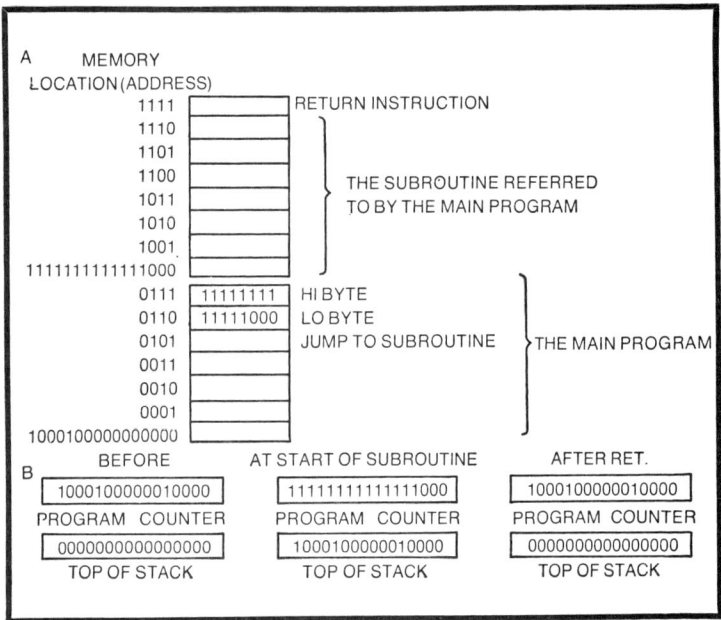

```
A     MEMORY
    LOCATION (ADDRESS)
              1111  ┌──────────┐  RETURN INSTRUCTION
              1110  │          │  ┐
              1101  │          │  │
              1100  │          │  │
              1011  │          │  │  THE SUBROUTINE REFERRED
              1010  │          │  │  TO BY THE MAIN PROGRAM
              1001  │          │  │
   1111111111111000 │          │  ┘
              0111  │ 11111111 │  HI BYTE      ┐
              0110  │ 11111000 │  LO BYTE      │
              0101  │          │  JUMP TO SUBROUTINE  ├ THE MAIN PROGRAM
              0011  │          │               │
              0010  │          │               │
              0001  │          │               ┘
   1000100000000000 └──────────┘
```

	BEFORE	AT START OF SUBROUTINE	AFTER RET.
B	1000100000010000	1111111111111000	1000100000010000
	PROGRAM COUNTER	PROGRAM COUNTER	PROGRAM COUNTER
	0000000000000000	1000100000010000	0000000000000000
	TOP OF STACK	TOP OF STACK	TOP OF STACK

Fig. 9-16. A memory diagram showing the sequence leading to a subroutine. When the JUMP TO SUBROUTINE instruction is fetched, the program counter is loaded with the next two words (see B).The stack now contains the original program counter value. When the RETURN instruction is fetched at the subroutine end, the original program counter value is from the stack into the program counter as shown at B.

instructions are different than CONDITIONAL or UNCONDITIONAL JUMP instructions.

JUMP TO SUBROUTINE OR CALL INSTRUCTIONS

The JUMP TO SUBROUTINE or CALL instructions differ from the CONDITIONAL and UNCONDITIONAL JUMP instructions because they cause the current value of the program counter to be saved on the top of the *stack*. Some of the microprocessors offer just a few JUMP TO SUBROUTINE and CONDITIONAL JUMP TO SUBROUTINE instructions. Other microprocessor instruction sets have as many UNCONDITIONAL and CONDITIONAL JUMP TO SUBROUTINE instructions as they have CONDITIONAL and UNCONDITIONAL JUMP instructions.

The programmer uses a JUMP TO SUBROUTINE instead of a JUMP when a return to the original program sequence is required (Fig. 9-16). A RETURN instruction is placed at the end of the subroutine (program) to get back to the main program. Some microprocessors have a simple return instruction that places the value at the top of the stack into the program counter. This causes the program counter to return to the original program sequence in effect when the subroutine was initiated. Other microprocessor instruction sets have many return instructions. These other return instructions are CONDITIONAL RETURN instructions. This means the return only occurs when a valid test of the status register is completed.

SPECIAL PROCESSOR INSTRUCTIONS

Each microprocessor has a series of instructions which are used to carry out special functions within that particular CPU. Some of these instructions are universal, others are unique to a particular microprocessor.

Almost all microprocessors have a HALT instruction. A *halt instruction* stops the processor. That is to say, the program counter is no longer incremented for each new processor cycle. Whether or not the processor actually stops or simply goes into a pseudo halt is dependent on the construction of the processor itself. Few processors are actually able to halt by stopping the clock. The clock is required to keep information stored in the registers.

The NOP *(no-operation)* instruction lets the processor go through one complete fetch/execute cycle without doing anything except using up time. The NOP instruction is often used when the programmer needs a short program delay.

Most microprocessors have the ability to be interrupted from the normal program sequence by an external event. The details of external interrupts are covered in Chapter 7. There are, however, standard instructions accompanying interrupt capability. Special instructions turn interrupt capability on and off, cause the processor to wait for an expected interrupt, cause the processor to return from an interrupt, and create software interrupts.

If the microprocessor has a stack in memory, there may be instructions to *push* and *pop* all register contents. These instructions are normally used in special subroutines such as when the microprocessor system detects a power failure.

Some microprocessors offer instructions to set or clear status register bits. These instructions are used by a programmer who must be sure the status register is initialized.

Other special instructions allow the programmer to swap data between two registers with one instruction. This can also be done using a few data transfer instructions. Some of the

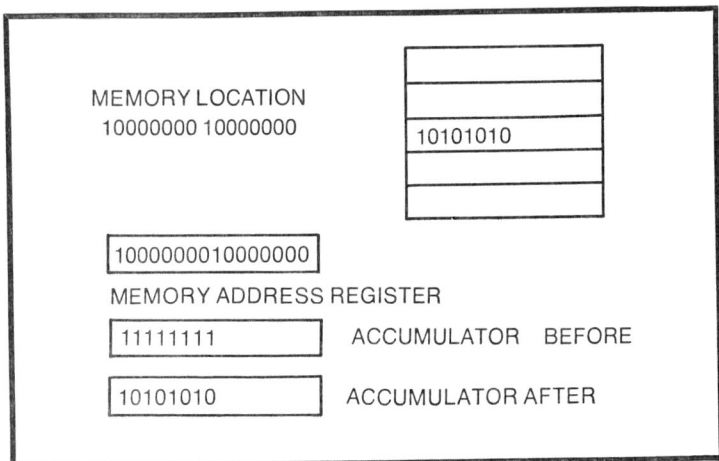

MEMORY LOCATION
10000000 10000000

10101010

1000000010000000

MEMORY ADDRESS REGISTER

11111111   ACCUMULATOR   BEFORE

10101010   ACCUMULATOR AFTER

Fig. 9-17. Using the indirect addressing mode to transfer memory contents at location 10000000010000000 to the accumulator. Note that the points to the location in memory for the data transfer instruction.

data swaps are used enough so time is saved if the job is done with a single instruction. *Swap* instructions are not limited to 8-bit swaps but may be used for 16-bit swaps in 8-bit microprocessors; for example, when swapping the program counter with the memory address register.

If the microprocessor does not treat an input/output device as a memory location, then a special instruction inputs data from an addressed input port. Another instruction outputs data to the addressed output port. Data going to or coming from an I/O device usually goes through the accumulator.

ADDRESSING MEMORY

The simplest and most common method of addressing memory is called *indirect addressing*. The memory address is indirectly specified by the register referred to in the instruction (usually the *memory address register*). When a memory transfer instruction is executed the processor uses the *memory address register* value to point to the desired memory lcoation. If the programmer wishes to transfer data with the next successive memory location the INCREMENT MEMORY ADDRESS REGISTER instruction is given, followed by the next transfer instruction. If a completely different point in memory is to be used the next transfer instruction must be preceded by an instruction to load a new value into the memory address register. Figure 9-17 shows a data transfer from memory location 1000000010000000 to the

138

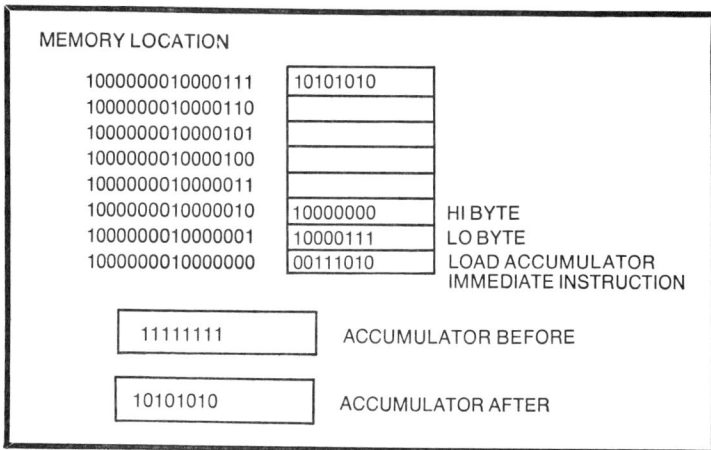

MEMORY LOCATION

1000000010000111	10101010	
1000000010000110		
1000000010000101		
1000000010000100		
1000000010000011		
1000000010000010	10000000	HI BYTE
1000000010000001	10000111	LO BYTE
1000000010000000	00111010	LOAD ACCUMULATOR IMMEDIATE INSTRUCTION

11111111	ACCUMULATOR BEFORE

10101010	ACCUMULATOR AFTER

Fig. 9-18. Using the direct addressing mode to transfer data from memory location 1000000010000111 to the accumulator. The load immediate instruction at memory location 1000.000010000000 is immediately followed by the LO and HI bytes of the data to be loaded into the accumulator. The before and after condition of the accumulator show its original contents 11111111 replaced by the 1000000010000111 memory location contents 10101010.

accumulator using indirect addressing. After the transfer is complete, the value of the accumulator has assumed the value 10101010. The contents of memory and the memory address register remain constant.

When *direct memory addressing* is used, the second and third instruction bytes contain the memory location address. An example of a DIRECT instruction is shown in Fig. 9-18.

Not all microprocessors are limited to addressing by indirect registers or direct addressing within the instruction. *Limited direct addressing* is a two byte instruction. The second byte contains the address. As the second byte is only eight bits long by definition, limited direct addressing only allows use of the lowest 256 words of memory. This is faster than three byte *direct addressing*, as only two bytes of information are fetched to complete the instruction. *Relative addressing* techniques also use a two-byte instruction. In these two-byte instructions the second byte is either added to or subtracted from the program counter or the memory address register. Once again, these modes of addressing offer a speed advantage as they require one less byte to be fetched. Relative addressing is limited, as the number combined with the program counter or the memory address register can only be eight bits long. Relative addressing permits the programmer to use a two-byte instruction to addresses anywhere in memory.

Chapter 10

Programming Concepts

Before writing a program for a microprocessor, the job for the microprocessor must be selected. The greatest effort in programming lies in clearly defining each step of the program. The job must be broken down into a series of *machine instructions*. These machine instructions must be written down in order and entered into the microprocessor memory. Certain rules of programming make the solution of the problem somewhat simpler. One of the easiest ways to define the job to be done is to draw a *flow chart*. A flow chart, such as that shown in Fig. 10-1, consists of a series of *blocks, circles*, and *diamonds* which represent the various activities that must be accomplished to complete the job. Once a flow chart of the job is complete, it may be expanded so each block in the flow chart represents one machine instruction for the particular microprocessor.

USING THE SERIES OF MACHINE INSTRUCTIONS

The programmer must know a variety of instructions and techniques to make efficient use of the microprocessor. The remainder of this chapter provides an introduction to these tools.

A Simple Sequential Program

The program which is flow charted in Fig. 10-2 is a simple straight line program. The program loads a number in the accumulator, adds a second number to the accumulator, and transfers the result to an indicated memory location. This is the simplest form of program. For each of the actual steps a

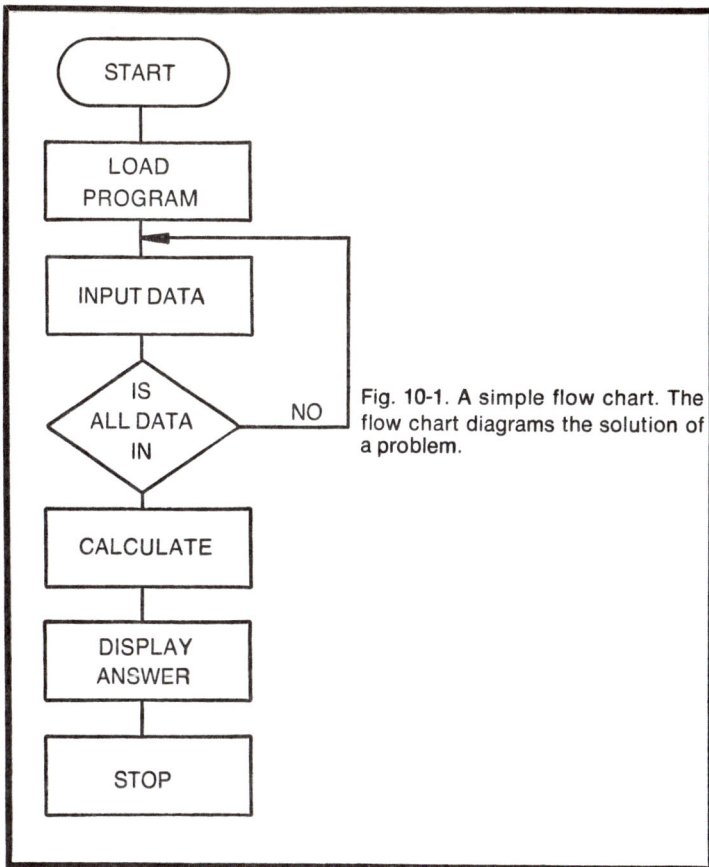

Fig. 10-1. A simple flow chart. The flow chart diagrams the solution of a problem.

machine instruction may be written down, as shown in Fig. 10-2. This series of binary numbers constitutes the actual program.

A Looped Program

More complex programs make use of a loop. The program diagram in Fig. 10-3 has a loop. This program is used to determine the size of memory attached to a microprocessor. The program operates as follows·

1. the accumulator is loaded with a 10101010;
2. the memory address register is cleared;
3. the memory location is loaded with the number in the accumulator;
4. the contents of the memory location are loaded into register B;

141

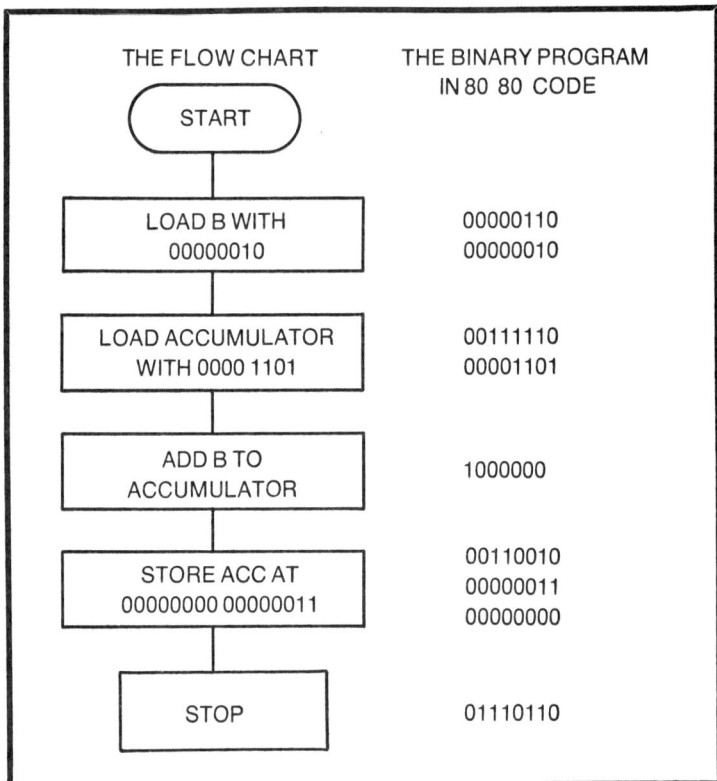

Fig. 10-2. A simple straight line program. This program loads a number in the accumulator, a second number in register B, adds them together and stores the results in memory location three. The binary numbers represent the actual machine code required to solve the problem. Note that some blocks on the flow chart only require one byte, some require two and others three.

5. the contents of the accumulator are compared to the contents of register B:

a. If the accumulator and register B are equal, there was memory at the addressed location. It accepted the 10101010 from the accumulator and transferred it to register B.

b. If the accumulator and register B are not equal, there was no memory at the addressed location. It did not accept the 10101010 from the accumulator and probably transferred either a 00000000 or a 11111111 to register B;

6. the program returns to the second step, incrementing the memory location if the two are found to be equal,

or halts if they are unequal. If they are unequal, we assume the memory address register was pointing to a nonvolatile section of memory.

This program has a *loop*. Until nonvolatile memory is found, the diamond test point returns the program to point three. The program remains in this loop until the test is not valid. *Looping* and *testing* are very important features of the microprocessor. Loops may be nested many many levels deep. However, loops may not cross over loops. This completely confuses the microprocessor and results in a meaningless program.

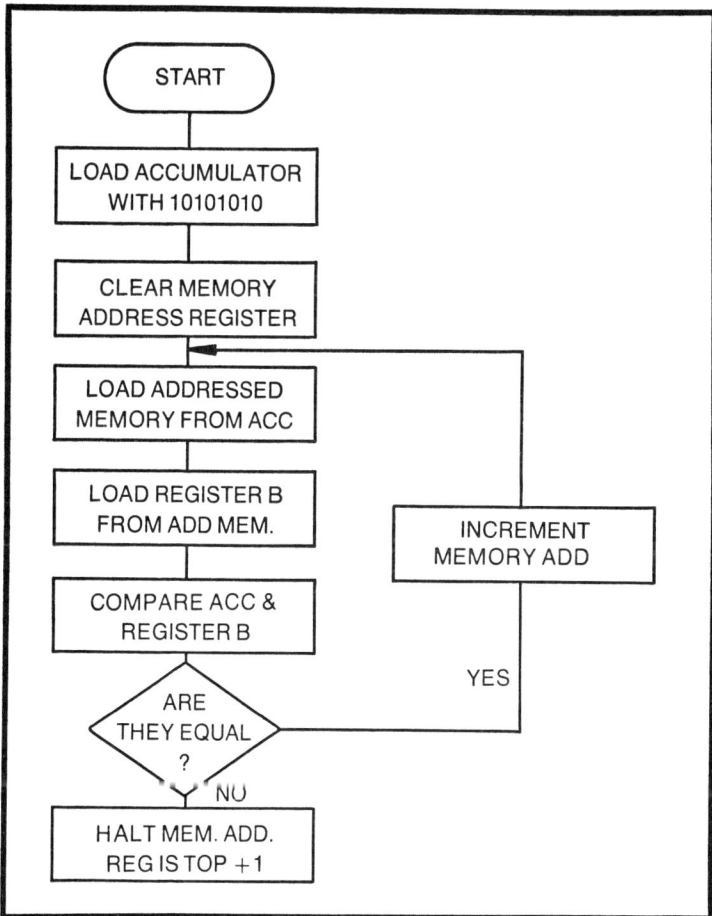

Fig. 10-3. A looped program. The memory test continues until the memory address register is incremented to a nonexistent location.

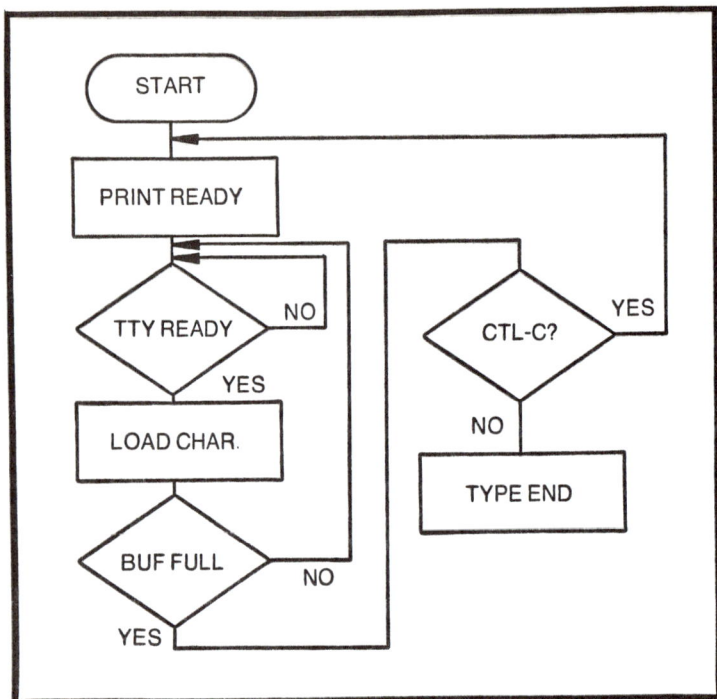

Fig. 10-4. Loops within loops. This program loads a test buffer or file. The first loop tests to see if the Teletype (TTY) is ready, the second loop tests to see if the buffer is full. The third loop looks to see if the typed character was a CONTROL -C (CTL-C) which aborts the text storage.

Using Subroutines

When writing a microprocessor program one portion of the program is often used many times. There is no point in writing this portion of the program over and over again. We therefore use a *subroutine*. That is, using a *call subroutine instruction*, a short portion of the program can be called from different points within the main program as many times as needed. Subroutines may call other subroutines. However, the number of subroutines which may be called from within subroutines is dependent upon the microprocessor being used. Calling a subroutine within a subroutine uses the stack. Therefore, the level of subroutine nesting is limited by the stack size. Figure 10-5 is a flow chart of a program employing two subroutines.

Creating the Instruction Set to Mnemonics

Mnemonics are short words or abbreviations used to represent certain instructions. Each microprocessor has a

144

certain set of designated mnemonics that go with the machine instructions. Mnemonics make programming simpler. It isn't necessary to remember the binary, octal, or hexidecimal numbers representing an instruction. For example, to CLear the Accumulator, CLA is all that is needed. To move the contents of memory into register B might be MOV A,M.

After the program is flow charted, the instruction sequence can be written in mnemonics. The programmer then turns to the microprocessor *instruction card*, looks up the appropriate binary, octal, or hexidecimal notation for the mnemonics. This is called *assembling the program*. The program is not assembled until all the details are worked out using the easy-to-remember mnemonics. Assembly may be performed in one of two ways. It may be *hand assembled* as described above, or *machine language programmed*, a more

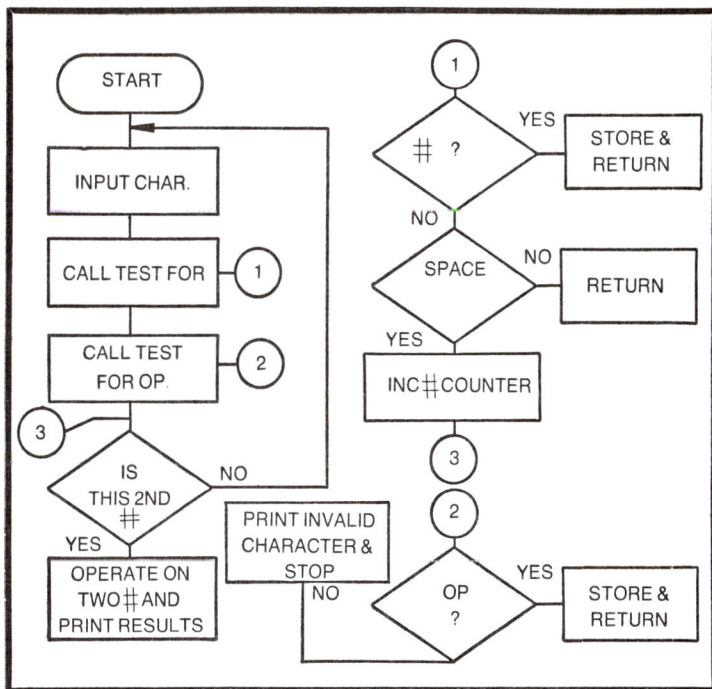

Fig. 10-5. A program using subroutines. This program inputs a character and uses a subroutine one to test for a number (⧣). The subroutine stores a number or looks for a space if it is not a number. If it is a space, it increments the number counter. A return from the first subroutine calls an operator (+ , − , × or ÷) test subroutine which stores the operator or aborts the program. After storing the operator, the program tests for two stored numbers. If there are, it computes and prints the results.

sophisticated method which actually handles the assembly. This machine assembly program is discussed in a later section.

Monitor Routines

Monitor routines (also known as *debug routines*) assist the programmer in perfecting the program once it is loaded. Few programs run perfectly the first time. They must be debugged. One way to debug the program is to use the front panel switch register and displays. Each location is examined and data is entered into those locations as necessary.

Another technique makes use of a *monitor program*. The monitor program permits the user to enter the memory address (in either octal or hexidecimal, depending on the monitor routine), and the contents of the addressed memory location is then displayed. By typing in an additional symbol, the user may *crack* the location and change the contents. Monitor packages permit the programmer to write and modify programs up to a few hundred steps in length relatively easily.

Well designed monitors usually include a *loader*. A loader loads previously recorded programs into memory. *Dump routines* are also included. A dump records the memory contents on a mass storage device, once the program is correct or is in a situation that the programmer wishes to prevent its destruction.

Advanced monitor packages may also include capability for *single stepping* and *break pointing*. Single stepping permits the user to cycle through the program, one instruction at a time. Break pointing permits the user to cycle through the program, passing a designated set of steps before the microprocessor halts. Break pointing is often quite useful when debugging long programs where single stepping is either too tedious or simply does not catch the problem.

Assemblers

Programming the microprocessor is significantly easier when an *assembler* is used. An assembler program takes a list of mnemonics and converts them into *binary machine language instructions*. In Fig. 10-6 this was done by hand using the operator's reference card for the microprocessor to look up the binary equivalents of the mnemonics. The assembler is primarily designed for use with moderately large programs. For short programs, it's just as simple to hand assemble the program and type it in, using a front panel as a monitor.

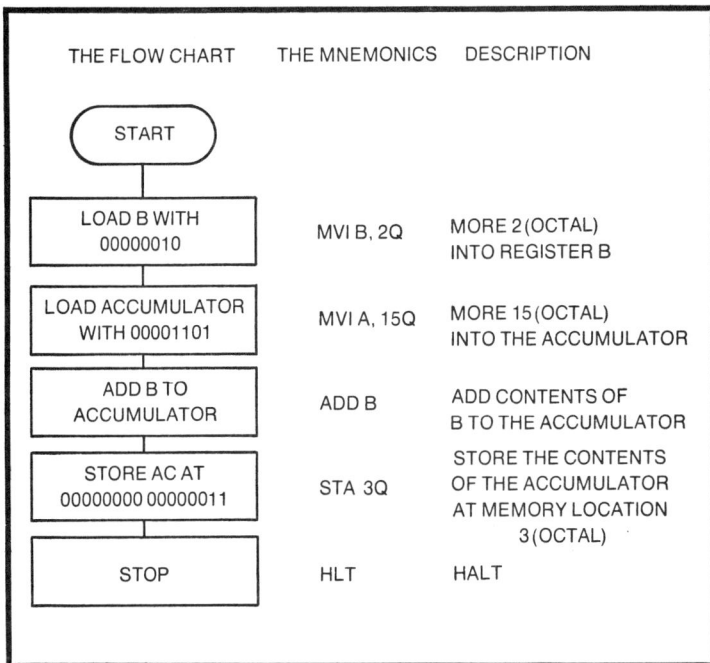

| THE FLOW CHART | THE MNEMONICS | DESCRIPTION |

THE FLOW CHART	THE MNEMONICS	DESCRIPTION
START		
LOAD B WITH 00000010	MVI B, 2Q	MORE 2(OCTAL) INTO REGISTER B
LOAD ACCUMULATOR WITH 00001101	MVI A, 15Q	MORE 15(OCTAL) INTO THE ACCUMULATOR
ADD B TO ACCUMULATOR	ADD B	ADD CONTENTS OF B TO THE ACCUMULATOR
STORE AC AT 00000000 00000011	STA 3Q	STORE THE CONTENTS OF THE ACCUMULATOR AT MEMORY LOCATION 3(OCTAL)
STOP	HLT	HALT

Fig. 10-6. The program from Fig. 10-2 with mnemonics substituted for the binary machine code

Assemblers have additional features which make writing a program simpler than machine language programming or hand assembly. Addresses may be given *symbolic names*. For example, a program with a loop must have a definite address to which the decision point jumps. In machine code programming, a specific numeric address is assigned to this location. In assembly language this location is given a symbolic name. The assembler converts the symbolic name to a numeric address.

The information supplied to the assembler (*code*) is generally given in a four column (field) format. These four columns are called *labels, op codes, operands*, and *comments*. The *label field* contains the symbolic names of referenced address. The *op code field* contains the mnemonics for the various microprocessor instructions to be used. The *operand field* contains the names of any registers, symbolic memory locations, etc., operated on by the instruction in the op code field. The *comments field* permits the programmer to document the program. A sample program written in assembly format with the four fields is shown in Fig. 10-7.

LABEL	OP CODE	OPERAND	COMMENTS
	ORG	0	Start the program at memory location 0.
	MVI	A, 10101010B	Load the accumulator with 10101010 binary.
	LXI	H, END+1	Load the H & L Register pair (the memory address register) with END+1 (e.g., start test at next location after this program.
LOOP	MOV	M, A	Move the contents of the accumulator into the memory location pointed to by H&L
	MOV	B, M	Move the contents of the H&L memory location into Register B.
	CMP	B	Compare accumulator and Register B, if equal set Z bit in status register to 1.
	JNZ	END	Jump to END, if Z is zero (A≠B) continue to next step if equal.
	INX	H	Increment H & L pair (the memory address register).
	JMP	LOOP	Jump to the address loop (keep going).
END	HALT		Stop program A≠B. H & L point to top of memory +1.

Fig. 10-7. The program of Fig. 10-3 (memory test) written in assembly code.

Assemblers come in two forms. A *resident* assembler may be loaded into the microprocessor itself. When the resident assembler is started, it usually reads the *source code* two or three times. Each time it reads, the source code is referred to as a pass. Most assemblers require multiple passes to get all the labels and operands straight. When the assembler is complete, an *object tape* is generated. The object tape is the binary output identical to the machine language program which could have been hand written. Of course, all the remarks are eliminated from the object tape, and symbolic addresses have been converted into fixed binary numbers representing actual microprocessor memory addresses.

Some assemblers produce a *symbol table*. The symbol table defines the points in the program at which all symbolic addresses are used and defines the binary, octal, or hexidecimal addresses assigned to that symbolic address.

Another form of assembler is called the *cross assembler*. The cross assembler does not reside within the microprocessor itself, but operates on another computer. However, it performs the same function. The advantage of cross assemblers is they may use a much more powerful computer, and therefore, they may be a more sophisticated assembler. If the resident assembler is not used with a microprocessor with a fairly large amount of memory (8K or more) the assembler has very limited capabilities.

Editors

An *editor* is a special program used to prepare assembler source code. The editor converts the microprocessor and a terminal into a sophisticated typewriter. The programmer may type in information for the label, op code, operand, and comment fields. If errors are made, the operator may correct these errors very easily using the features of the editor. Once again, editors may be resident on the microprocessor or resident on another computer. The more powerful editors require moderately large memory space (8K or more) and are therefore restricted to use on large microprocessor systems or small minicomputers.

HIGH LEVEL LANGUAGES

When using all previous forms of programming, a line of program code must be prepared for each machine instruction the microprocessor is to carry out. That is, to add two numbers in the accumulator, the first number must be added to it and then the result must be moved to the desired memory location. Needless to say, this is a great deal of work to do a simple job, such as adding two numbers which lie in the range of +127 to −127.

In order to simplify the process of writing programs containing complex mathematical manipulations, a number of high-level programs have been written. These high-level programs permit the operator to enter an expression such as PRINT 31 + 64 and the microprocessor responds with the answer 95.

This simple addition problem required many many lines of machine language code to solve the problem. The more sophisticated program took the simple command PRINT 31 + 64 and reduced it to the appropriate series of machine language instructions, carried out the computations and printed the answer. Obviously, most of the problems to be solved are much greater than simply adding two numbers together. Long programs containing many lines of high-level language-source code may be written.

There are two different types of programs which reduce the source code to machine instructions. The simpler and slower program is called an *interpretive language*. The faster and more complex program is called a *compiler*. The difference between an interpreter and a compiler is in how they convert the source code into machine instructions.

The interpretive language interprets each line of the source code, a single line at a time, and executes all instructions on the line before moving on to the next line. The interpreter executes the line of source code by calling many subroutines from its library. If there is a problem on the 25th line, that problem is not recognized until the 25th line is executed.

On the other hand, the compiler creates a complete set of machine instructions to solve the problem before the program is executed. That is to say, the entire problem is converted to an appropriate set of machine language instructions which are then reloaded into the computer and executed. Interpretive languages are shown and always use the same amount of memory. The interpreter with its great library of subroutines must always be present in memory to execute the program. On the other hand, while the final object code from a compiler may be quite short when compared to the interpreter itself, the compiler is a very extensive program. In fact, compilers require so much memory space, few have ever been written for microprocessors.

The widely used language BASIC is an interpretive language. That is, it solves the problems line by line as it works its way through the program. FORTRAN is a compiler, and the entire program must be written correctly and compiled prior to running the program. Compiling the program converts the FORTRAN source code into a binary object program, in much the same manner as an assembler converts an assembly source code into a binary object program.

DIAGNOSTIC PROGRAMS

A special series of programs is available for most microprocessors or microprocessor systems which fall under the heading of *diagnostics*. Diagnostics programs are exactly what their name implies. They are used to diagnose difficulties with the microprocessor or its associated components. For example, one diagnostic program might check proper operation of the microprocessor instruction set. Other microprocessor diagnostic programs check for proper operation of serial I/O ports, parallel I/O ports, and memory. Memory diagnostics are particularly valuable because this is an area which the hobbyist and home experimenter is frequently adding to, and therefore, an area frequently prone to hardware errors.

Chapter 11

Two Microprocessors–

The 6800 and the 8080

The 6800 and the 8080 are two very popular 8-bit microprocessors. The 8080 is a *second generation* microprocessor. That is, it is a more powerful version of the original 8008 microprocessor introduced by Intel in the early 1970s. The 6800 has no real predecessor, but it is second generation architecture.

Both the 6800 and the 8080 are capable of addressing 65K words of memory. Both have comparable speeds, and both use an 8-bit *bidirectional data bus*. The 6800 and the 8080 are supported by expensive software at all levels. Both microprocessors are used as the basis of a number of different personal or hobbyist microcomputers.

This chapter looks at each of these microprocessors. The various input and output integrated circuit connections are explained in terms developed earlier in this book. The architecture of each microprocessor is discussed, and the end of the chapter compares the two microprocessors. This chapter also discusses some of the support circuits required by each microprocessor.

Both the 6800 and the 8080 are excellent microprocessors. Between the two of them, all the major architectural concepts used in most microprocessors are illustrated. In order to get the most from this chapter, *briefly* read through to become acquainted with both the 6800 and the 8080. After a fast reading, a second reading of the chapter provides a much better understanding of the differences between the 6800 and the 8080 and the significant architectural points of each.

THE MOTOROLA 6800

The original 6800 was introduced by Motorola. At the present time, a number of semiconductor manufacturers are licensed to manufacture 6800 microprocessors. The block diagram of Fig. 11-1 shows the internal construction of the 6800. Some of the 6800's outstanding features are:

- memory and I/O are treated identically;
- +5 volt (single supply voltage) operation;
- two independent and complete 8-bit accumulators;
- a 16-bit program counter;
- a 16-bit stack pointer;
- a 16-bit index register;
- an internal 8-bit data bus to transfer data between registers, the arithmetic and logic unit, and the input/output data bus latch;
- op codes and memory addresses are usually expressed in hexidecimal.

Referring to Fig. 11-1, all 40 pins of the dual-in-line package are used. The following list briefly describes the function of these various lines.

1. The single biggest group of lines is the 16 address lines. They are permanently latched by the LO byte buffer and the HI byte buffer. However, the outputs are tristateable.
2. The next largest group of lines is the 8-bit bidirectional data bus. These eight lines contain data coming from or going into the 6800.
3. Positive 5 volt power is supplied on pin 8, and ground (return) is supplied to pins 1 and 21.
4. The 6800 requires a two-phase nonoverlapping clock. These two signals are shown on the left hand side of Fig. 11-1, entering the instruction decode and control block.
5. The $\overline{HALT}$ line stops the processor fetch/execute operation when this line is asserted.
6. The *three-state control* line produces a tri-state condition on the address and data lines. It also forces the valid memory address and bus available lines low.
7. The *read/write* line signals memory when the 6800 is placing data on the 8-bit bidirectional data lines (write) or it is ready to receive data on the 8-bit directional lines (read).
8. The *valid memory address* line tells memory the address data on the address lines is valid.

153

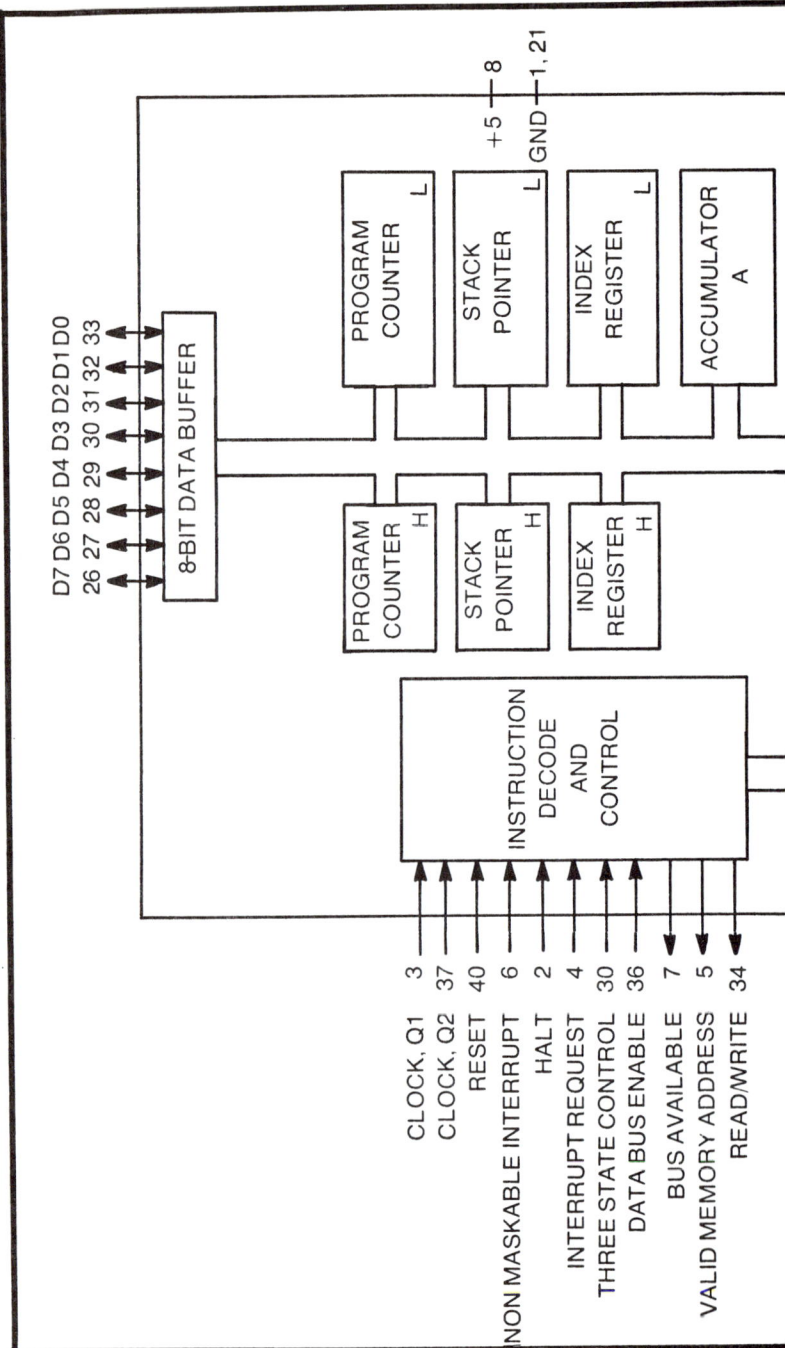

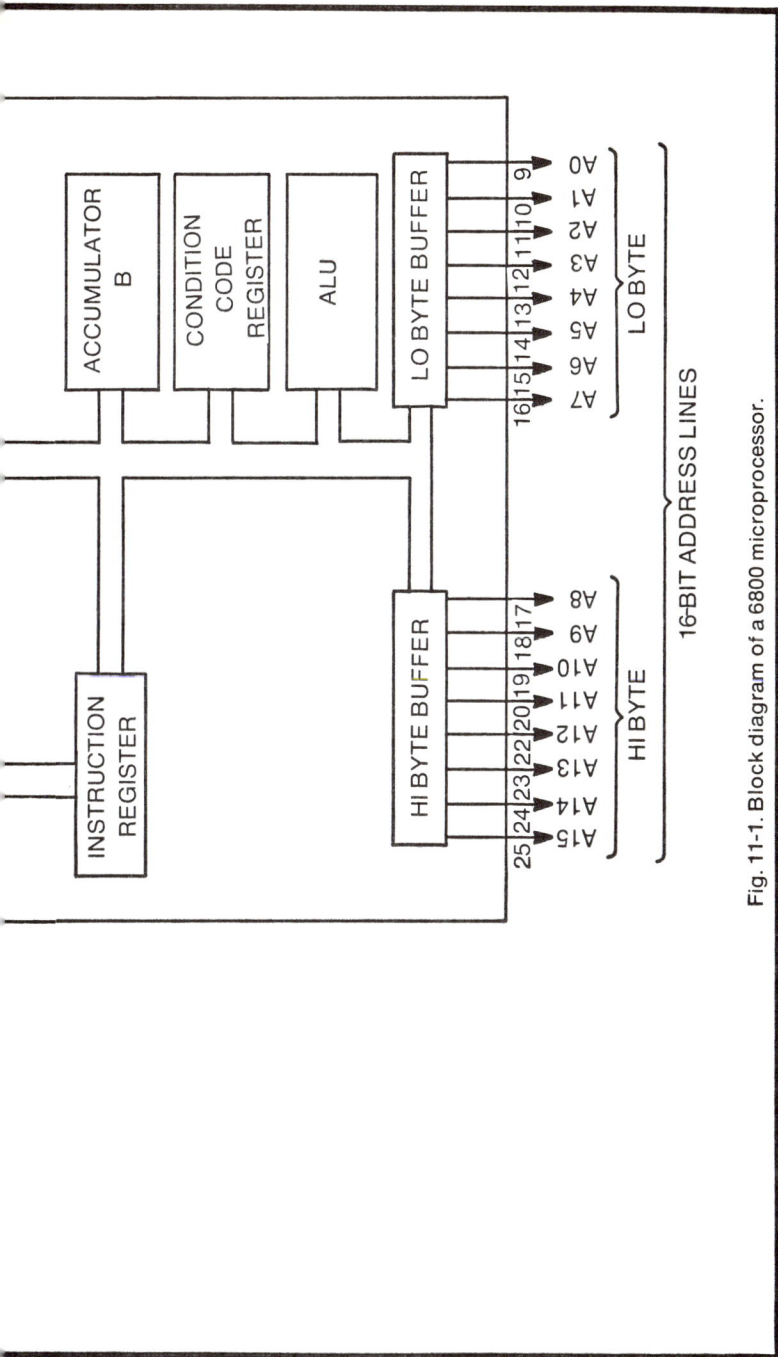

Fig. 11-1. Block diagram of a 6800 microprocessor.

9. The *data bus enable* line enables the output of the 8-bit data buffer. It causes the bus available to go high, indicating the microprocessor is stopped and the address bus is available for use by an external device.

10. The *Interrupt Request* line (IRQ) requests an interrupt sequence be started within the 6800. The 6800 completes its current instruction cycle and then a 16-bit address points to memory locations FFF8 and FFF9 (hexidecimal). Normally an address is stored at these memory locations (vectors) which starts a subroutine servicing the device, causing the interrupt.

11. The $\overline{RESET}$ input starts the 6800 when it is powered up. When this line is asserted the processor completes its current instruction cycle (if it is executing one) and then vectors to the last two memory locations (FFFE and FFFF hexidecimal). The contents of these vectors contain the starting addresses for a power up subroutine.

12. The *Non-Maskable Interrupt* ($\overline{NMI}$) is a second input which may request an interrupt sequence to start. This interrupt sequence vectors to memory locations FFFC and FFFD. The nonmaskable interrupt differs from the interrupt request line as the 6800 may not be programmed to ignore this interrupt. It can be programmed to ignore a request on the $\overline{IRQ}$ line.

The 6800 offers one additional interrupt. This is called a *software interrupt*. The software interrupt vectors to locations FFFA and FFFB. Using the software interrupt, the programmer may cause a particular program or data condition to interrupt the processor's instruction sequence.

Table 11-1 shows the various memory locations used for interrupt vectors in the 6800. Again, each vector can point to a subroutine which may be as long as required to service the particular interrupt.

Table 11-1. Memory Vectors for the 6800's Four Interrupts.

VECTOR		DESCRIPTION
HI BYTE	LO BYTE	
FFFE	FFFF	Restart
FFFC	FFFD	Non-Maskable Interrupt
FFFA	FFFB	Software Interrupt
FFF8	FFF9	Interrupt Request

The 6800 microprocessor has 72 different instructions in its instruction set. These 72 different instructions are listed in alphabetical order in Table 11-2. This table shows the mnemonics and a brief description of the instruction.

These 72 different instructions are augmented by different address modes of the 6800. Any of the 6800's instructions involving addressing a memory location or an accumulator may address the memory location or the accumulator by one or more of the seven different address modes. In effect, this expands the instruction set considerably.

The seven different address modes are:

1. *accumulator addressing.* A single byte instruction address either accumulator A or accumulator B;
2. *immediate addressing.* The data word to be processed is the second byte of the instruction. If the LDS or LDX instructions are being executed, they are 3-byte instructions. The second and third byte of the instruction contain the data to be placed in the stack pointer (LDS) or the index register (LDX);
3. *direct addressing.* The data to be processed is contained at the address specified in the second byte of the instruction. Using the direct address mode, the programmer may address 256 memory locations ($2^8 = 256$). These are the lowest 256 bytes of 6800 memory. The purpose of direct addressing is to provide short instructions, thus increasing speed;
4. *extended addressing.* Extended addressing is very similar to direct addressing except data to be operated on is contained in the address location, pointed to by the second and third bytes of the 3-byte instruction. Using extended addressing, the programmer may address any memory location within the full 65K range of the 6800 microprocessor;
5. *indexed addressing.* Indexed addressing uses the 16-bit binary number stored in the index register. The second byte of the instruction is added to the current value of the lower 8-bits of the index register. The resultant 16-bit number is then used to address the desired memory location;
6. *implied addressing.* Implied addressing points to any one of the 6800's registers. This accumulator addressing is a special form of implied addressing which only uses the accumulators;
7. *relative addressing.* Relative addressing uses the current value contained in the 16-bit program counter.

Table 11-2. Instruction Set for the 6800.

ABA	Add Accumulators
ADC	Add with Carry
ADD	Add
AND	Logical And
ASL	Arithmetic Shift Left
ASR	Arithmetic Shift Right
BCC	Branch if Carry Clear
BCS	Branch if Carry Set
BEQ	Branch if Equal to Zero
BGE	Branch if Greater or Equal Zero
BGT	Branch if Greater than Zero
BHI	Branch if Higher
BIT	Bit Test
BLE	Branch if Less or Equal
BLS	Branch if Lower or Same
BLT	Branch if Less than Zero
BMI	Branch if Minus
BNE	Branch if Not Equal to Zero
BPL	Branch if Plus
BRA	Branch Always
BSR	Branch to Subroutine
BVC	Branch if Overflow Clear
BVS	Branch if Overflow Set
CBA	Compare Accumulators
CLC	Clear Carry
CLI	Clear Interrupt Mask
CLR	Clear
CLV	Clear Overflow
CMP	Compare
COM	Complement
CPX	Compare Index Register
DAA	Decimal Adjust
DEC	Decrement
DES	Decrement Stack Pointer
DEX	Decrement Index Register
EOR	Exclusive OR
INC	Increment
INS	Increment Stack Pointer
INX	Increment Index Register
MJP	Jump
JSR	Jump to Subroutine
LDA	Load Accumulator
LDS	Load Stack Pointer
LDX	Load Index Register
LSR	Logical Shift Right
NEG	Negate

Table 11-2. Cont.

NOP	No Operation
ORA	Inclusive OR Accumulator
PSH	Push Data
PUL	Pull Data
ROL	Rotate Left
ROR	Rotate Right
RTI	Return from Interrupt
RTS	Return from Subroutine
SBA	Subtract Accumulators
SBC	Subtract with Carry
SEC	Set Carry
SEI	Set Interrupt Mask
SEV	Set Overflow
STA	Store Accumulator
STS	Store Stack Register
STX	Store Index Register
SUB	Subtract
SWI	Software Interrupt
TAB	Transfer Accumulators
TAP	Transfer Accumulators to Condition Code Reg.
TBA	Transfer Accumulators
TPA	Transfer Condition Code Reg. to Accumulator
TST	Test
TSX	Transfer Stack Pointer to Index Register
TXS	Transfer Index Register to Stack Pointer
WA1	Wait for Interrupt

The second byte of an instruction is added to the lowest 8-bits of the program counter (plus 2). Relative addressing allows the programmer to address memory locations within the range of +129 bytes to −125 bytes of the present instruction location. Relative addressing is a 2-byte instruction.

ALU operations in the 6800 affect the 6-bits of the condition code register. The condition code register or status register in the 6800 reflects the following conditions:

- Bit 0. This bit is set by a carry from bit 7;
- Bit 1. This bit is set when a two's complement arithmetic operation generates an overflow;
- Bit 2. This bit is set when the operation results in a byte containing all zeros;
- Bit 3. This bit is set when the operation results in a one in the most significant bit. That is to say, the answer is negative;

- Bit 4. This bit is an interrupt mask, and when set, the interrupt request is disabled;
- Bit 5. This bit is a half carry from bit 3, and is used to assist in decimal arithmetic.

THE INTEL 8080

As noted in the introduction, the 8080 is Intel's second generation 8-bit microprocessor. Its predecessor is the 8008 and, in many ways, the 8080 is simply a super 8008. At the present time a number of semiconductor manufacturers are licensed to manufacture 8080 microprocessors. Figure 11-2 is a block diagram of the 8080. Comparing Fig. 11-2 to Fig. 11-1, one can see many of the similarities and many of the differences between the 8080 and the 6800. The 8080 treats I/O devices as unique addresses. That is to say, the 8080 has a separate I/O instruction. Therefore, the 8080 can address a 65K of memory, 256 input devices and 256 output devices. Some of the 8080's outstanding features are:

- three volt operation using +12, +5, and −5 volt supplies;
- a 16-bit program counter;
- a 16-bit stack pointer;
- a single 8-bit accumulator;
- six registers configured as 3-register pairs, the BC pair, the DE pair, and the HL pair. The HL pair are used as the memory address register;
- an internal 8-bit data bus to transfer data between registers, the arithmetic logic unit, and the input/output data buses latch; and
- op codes and addresses are frequently given in either octal or hexidecimal.

The following paragraphs briefly reviews the 8080's connection to the outside world.

1. The biggest group of lines are the address lines. Sixteen-lines are required, so the 8080 can address a full 65K. The address lines are not latched. Therefore, address information is only momentarily available.
2. The next biggest group of lines is the eight data lines which carry bidirectional data to and from memory and input/output devices. The 8080 data lines also carry a status word during a portion of the fetch/execute cycle. This status word must be latched at a certain time during the operation of the fetch/execute cycle, and decoded. The decoded

information from the status word tells the 8080 external circuits the mode the 8080 is presently operating in. For example, it identifies input instructions versus output instructions. The status word also signals memory read/write conditions. If an interrupt is involved, the status word also plays a special role.

3. As noted earlier, the 8080 required +12 volts, +5 volts, and −5 volts, and ground.

4. The *write signal* ($\overline{WR}$) indicates stable data on the data bus during an output transfer.

5. The *data bus in-signal*, ($\overline{DBIN}$) indicates the data bus is in an input mode. This signal is used to permit information to enter the 8080.

6. The *Interrupt Request Line* (INT) generates an interrupt sequence within the 8080. When an interrupt is generated, external logic must apply a data word to the processor via the 8-bit bidirectional data lines. This special data word starts the microprocessor at seven different memory locations (10, 20, 30, 40, 50, 60, and 70 octal). This gives the 8080 seven different interrupt vectors.

7. The *Interrupt Enable* (INTE) signal tells external logic whether or not the 8080 will accept an interrupt. Interrupt capability with the 8080 may be turned on or shut off by the programmer.

8. The *HoLD* (HLD) signal requests the 8080 to enter a special state. This state allows an external device to gain control of the 8080 address and data bus, as soon as the 8080 completes its current cycle. The hold signal is used to facilitate Direct Memory Access (DMA).

9. The *HoLd Acknowledge* (HLDA) output shows the 8080 is responding to a hold signal. The hold acknowledge signal indicates the data in address bus is in the tristate mode.

10. The *ready signal* is an input line used by memory or I/O to signal the 8080 when valid input data is available on the data bus. The signal synchronizes the 8080 with slow memory or I/O devices. When the 8080 sends an address, and does not receive a ready input, it enters the wait state until the ready signal is given.

11. The *wait signal* indicates the 8080 is in the wait state.

12. The *SYNChronizing signal* (SYNC) indicates the beginning of each of the main fetch/execute cycle.

13. The 8080 requires a two-phase nonoverlapping clock.

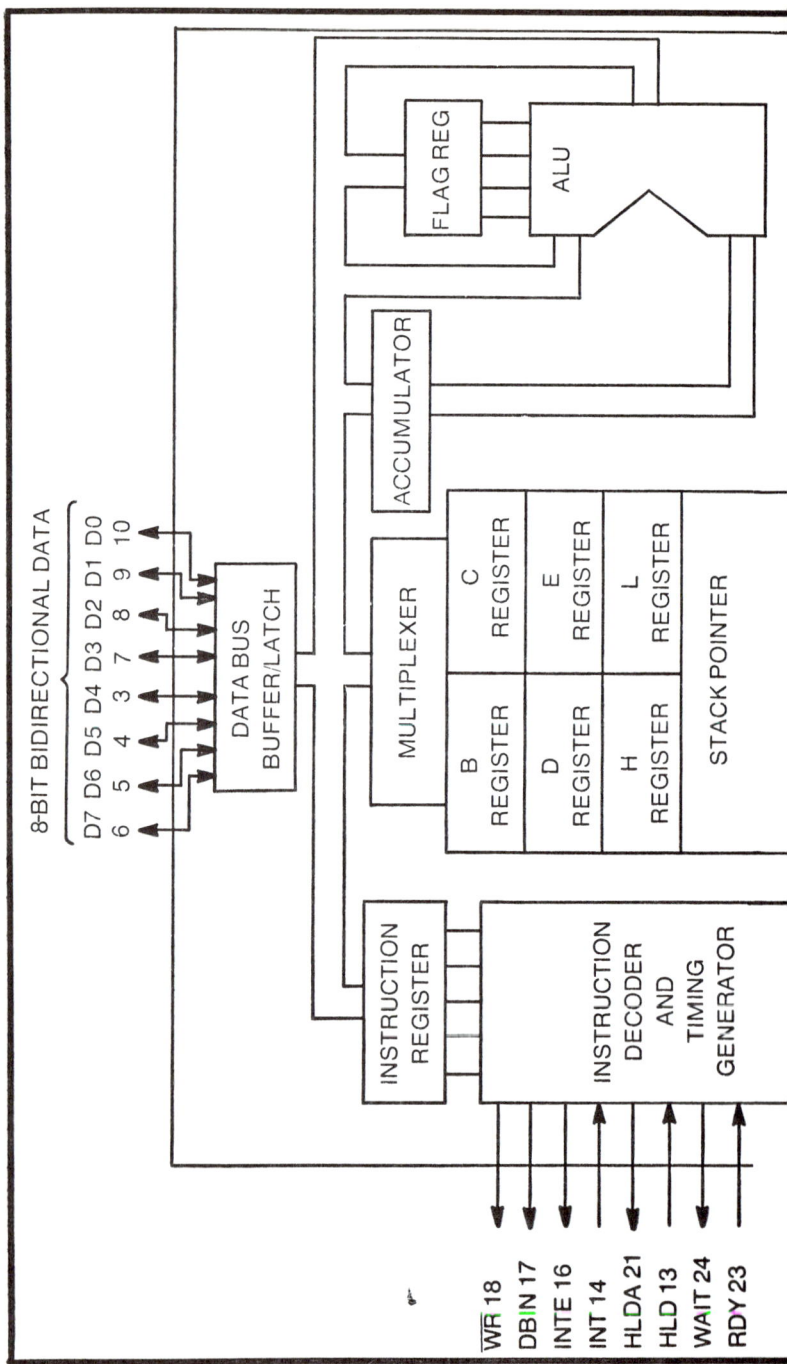

8-BIT BIDIRECTIONAL DATA

D7 D6 D5 D4 D3 D2 D1 D0
6 5 4 3 7 8 9 10

DATA BUS BUFFER/LATCH

FLAG REG

ALU

ACCUMULATOR

MULTIPLEXER

B REGISTER	C REGISTER
D REGISTER	E REGISTER
H REGISTER	L REGISTER
STACK POINTER	

INSTRUCTION REGISTER

INSTRUCTION DECODER AND TIMING GENERATOR

WR 18
DBIN 17
INTE 16
INT 14
HLDA 21
HLD 13
WAIT 24
RDY 23

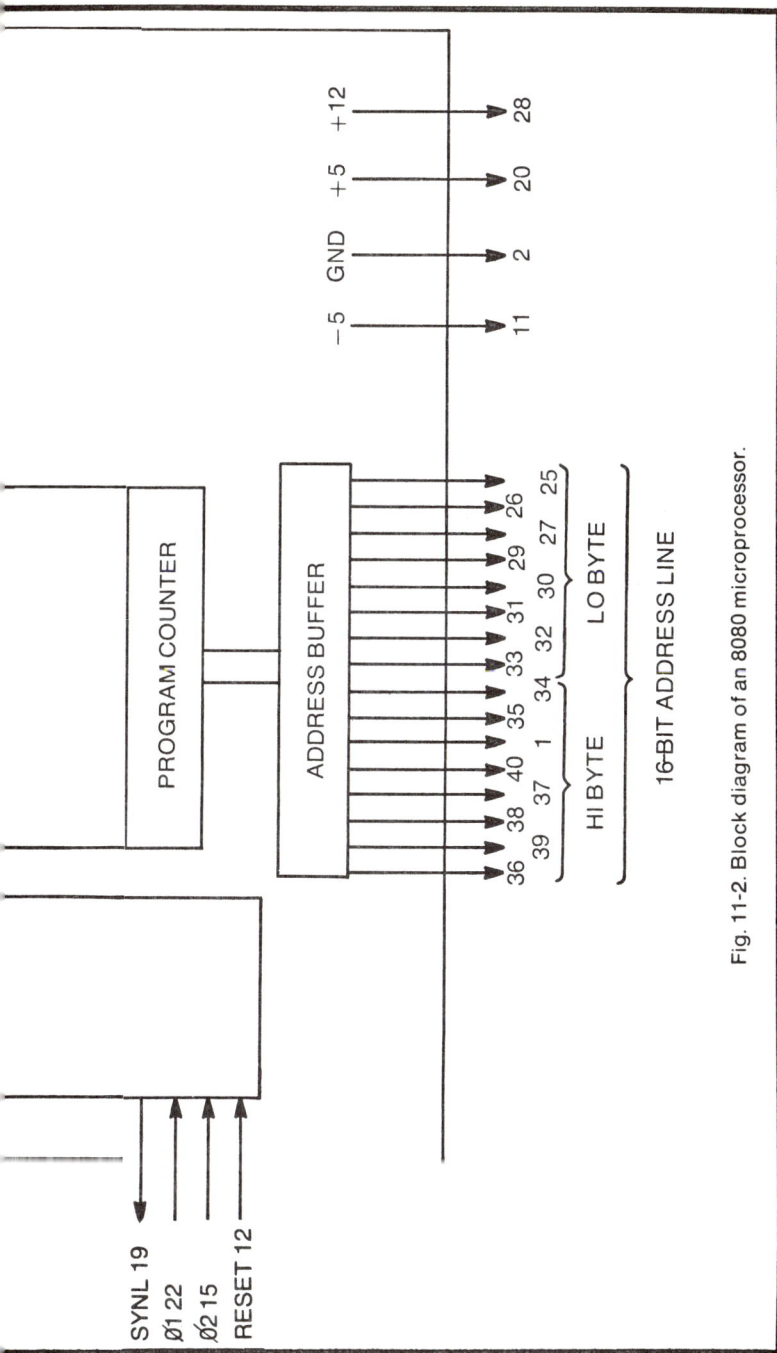

Fig. 11-2. Block diagram of an 8080 microprocessor.

Table 11-3. Instruction Set for the 8080.

MOV r_1, r_2	Move register to register
MOV M, r	Move register to memory
MOV r, M	Move memory to register
HLT	Halt
MVI r	Move immediate register
MVI M	Move immediate memory
INR r	Increment register
DCR r	Decrement register
INR M	Increment memory
DCR M	Decrement memory
ADD r	Add register to A
ADC r	Add register to A with carry
SUB r	Subtract register from A
SBB r	Subtract register from A with borrow
ANA r	And register with A
XRA r	Exclusive Or register with A
ORA r	Or register with A
CMP r	Compare register with A
ADD M	Add memory to A
ADC M	Add memory to A with carry
SUB M	Subtract memory from A
SBB M	Subtract memory from A with borrow
ANA M	And memory with A
XRA M	Exclusive Or memory with A
ORA M	Or memory with A
CMP M	Compare memory with A
ADI	Add immediate to A
ACI	Add immediate to A with carry
SUI	Subtract immediate from A
SBI	Subtract immediate from A with borrow
ANI	And immediate with A
XRI	Exclusive Or imediate with A
ORI	Or immediate with A
CPI	Compare immediate with A
RLC	Rotate A left
RRC	Rotate A right
RAL	Rotate A left through carry
RAR	Rotate A right through carry
JMP	Jump unconditional
JC	Jump on carry
JNC	Jump on no carry
JZ	Jump on zero
JNZ	Jump on no zero
JP	Jump on positive
JM	Jump on minus
JPE	Jump on parity even
JPO	Jump on parity odd
CALL	Call unconditional
CC	Call on carry
CNC	Call on no carry
CZ	Call on zero
CNZ	Call on no zero
CP	Call on positive
CM	Call on minus
CPE	Call on parity even
CPO	Call on parity odd
RET	Return
RC	Return on carry
RNC	Return on no carry
RZ	Return on zero
RNZ	Return on no zero
RP	Return on positive

Table 11-3. Cont.

RM	Return on minus
RPE	Return on parity even
RPO	Return on parity odd
RST	Restart
IN	Input
OUT	Output
LXI B	Load immediate register Pair B & C
LXI D	Load immediate register Pair D & E
LXI H	Load immediate register Pair H & L
LXI SP	Load immediate stack pointer
PUSH B	Push register Pair B & C on stack
PUSH D	Push register Pair D & E on stack
PUSH H	Push register Pair H & L on stack
PUSH PSW	Push A and Flags on stack
POP B	Pop register pair B & C off stack
POP D	Pop register pair D & E off stack
POP H	Pop register pair H & L off stack
POP PSW	Pop A and Flags off stack
STA	Store A direct
LDA	Load A direct
XCHG	Exchange D & E, H & L Registers
XTHL	Exchange top of stack, H & L
SPHL	H & L to stack pointer
PCHL	H & L to program counter
DAD B	Add B & C to H & L
DAD D	Add D & E to H & L
DAD H	Add H & L to H & L
DAD SP	Add stack pointer to H & L
STAX B	Store A indirect
STAX D	Store A indirect
LDAX B	Load A indirect
LDAX D	Load A indirect
INX B	Increment B & C registers
INX D	Increment D & E registers
INX H	Increment H & L registers
INX SP	Increment stack pointer
DCX B	Decrement B & C
DCX D	Decrement D & E
DCX H	Decrement H & L
DCX SP	Decrement stack pointer
CMA	Complement A
STC	Set carry
CMC	Complement carry
DAA	Decimal adjust A
SHLD	Store H & L direct
LHLD	Load H & L direct
EI	Enable Interrupts
DI	Disable interrupt
NOP	No-operation

14. The *reset signal* prepares the 8080 for initial operation. Reset zeros the program counter and the interrupt enabling flip-flop, and the hold acknowledge flip-flops are both reset. The ready input is a vectored interrupt to location 00.

Table 11-3 shows the 8080 instruction set giving the mnemonics and the English equivalents. These 111 instructions are augmented to some degree by different memory addressing techniques. The 8080 uses 1-byte, 2-byte, and 3-byte instructions.

The 8080 single byte instructions typically contain such commands as register-to-register data transfers, memory reference instructions (instructions using the HL register pair as the memory address register), arithmetic and logical instructions, stack instructions, and interrupt control instructions.

The double byte instructions are either immediate or I/O instructions. The immediate instructions load a register or a memory location with the contents of the second byte of the instruction. The I/O instructions direct an input or output from a designated I/O port.

Triple byte instructions are jump instructions, subroutine call instructions, or direct load instructions. The first byte contains the op code, the second byte contains the low address byte or operand #1 and the third byte contains the high address byte or operand #2. The second and third bytes are therefore either a memory address or data for the program counter.

Because of its extensive register structure, the 8080 has some unique instructions. For example, the programmer may use the six registers independently or the registers may be used as three register-pairs. When the registers are used as a pair, any arithmetic array from the low byte automatically affects the high byte if a carry is generated. However, when the registers are used independently, changes in the low byte have no affect on the high byte.

COMPARING THE 6800 AND THE 8080

The block diagrams of the 6800 and 8080, as well as their respective instruction sets, allow a very complete comparison of these two microprocessors. As noted earlier, the 6800 does not recognize separate I/O instructions. The 8080, on the other hand, has an additional 512 input/output instructions. The 6800 has two powerful 8-bit accumulators. The 8080 has a single accumulator, but the three register-pairs serve as more than simple memory.

The debate questioning the wisdom of a register oriented microprocessor versus an accumulator oriented micro-processor will continue for some time. It is primarily a function of the programming capabilities of the person using the microprocessor. Both microprocessors are used to perform very major tasks.

One should note when comparing the 6800 and the 8080 that simply counting the instruction set mnemonics given in Tables

11-1 and 11-2 is not a fair comparison of these two processors. The 6800 has extensive addressing modes, which effectively expand the instruction set. On the other hand, the 8080 has a larger number of basic instructions amplified by the many different registers involved.

REQUIRED SUPPORT

Neither the 6800 nor the 8080 is capable of stand-alone operation. Both microprocessors require a two-phase nonoverlapping clock. In both cases, this clock is probably generated by a special integrated circuit designed for the purpose. In addition to the clock circuit, the 8080 operates most efficiently when combined with a *system controller IC*. A system controller analyzes the status word which is presented on the data bus during the early portion of the fetch/execute cycle. It determines whether the microprocessor is in a memory or input/output mode and whether it is reading or writing. The system controller also assists in arbitrating interrupt requests. The 6800 does not require such a system controller.

Both the 6800 and the 8080 require external memory, external I/O port ICs, and external devices to buffer the data and address bus if any extensive amounts of memory or other devices are to be connected.

Chapter 12

Getting Started
With Microprocessors

By this time you are ready to start using your own micro-processor. The way you approach using a micropro-cessor is highly dependent on what you want to do with it, and what you can afford. This chapter discusses the three basic alternatives available to the home experimenter. You may elect a do-it-yourself system, an evaluation board, or a complete microcomputer. The purpose of this chapter is to briefly outline the major factors involved in these three alternatives. Of course, each one has its advantages and its disadvantages and each is suited to a slightly different purpose.

BREADBOARDING

Using a breadboard such as the one as shown in Fig. 12-1 is probably the lowest cost way to experiment with microprocessors. Breadboards, complete with power supplies, are available for less than $100. The integrated circuits, including the microprocessor itself, are available from many of the surplus semiconductor houses which regularly advertise in the hobbyist electronic magazines.

Generally speaking, systems built on a breadboard have limited functions, however, they give you an extremely good feel for how the hardware goes together. If you build a microprocessor system using a breadboard, you must study each of the microprocessor signals quite closely in order to produce a working system by connecting the microprocessor to its associated integrated circuits. There are a number of

168

Fig. 12-1. An IC breadboard. The ET-3300 provides sockets for many ICs ±12V and +5V. Photo courtesy Heath Company.

magazine articles describing such breadboard microprocessor configurations, and of course, there are always manufacturers' application notes.

In order to make the microprocessor breadboard valuable you must have an input and output device. A simple switch register, and an LED display is usually the most convenient when working with a breadboard. The breadboard must be wired so program information may be stored in memory. Once the program is stored in the memory, the memory must then be connected to the microprocessor to execute the program.

If you are breadboarding a 6800 system, a few minimum components are required. The breadboard must supply +5 volts, in the 1 to 2 ampere range. The breadboard sockets must accept 50-pin DIP ICs. In addition to the 6800 microprocessor the following ICs are helpful:

1. a clock generator
2. a bus compatible random access memory
3. a peripheral interface adaptor (a bus compatible parallel I/O port)
4. a read only memory preprogrammed with a monitor routine

If you are breadboarding an 8080 system, the breadboard must be able to supply +5 volts in a 1 to 2 ampere region, +12 volts at a few hundred mA, and −5 volts in the 10 mA range.

The breadboard sockets must be capable of accepting 40-pin DIP ICs. In addition to the 8080 microprocessor, the following ICs are helpful:

1. a clock generator
2. a system controller
3. bus compatible random access memory
4. an I/O peripheral interface IC; and
5. a preprogrammed ROM with a monitor routine

Breadboarding a microprocessor system is very instructional. This is especially true when hardware considerations are taken into account, for it is highly unlikely a breadboard will work the first time and considerable effort will be spent diagnosing wiring errors or other hardware problems. This time should not be considered a wasted effort if you are interested in learning about microprocessor hardware. Diagnosing difficulties in a breadboard is one of the best ways to learn how the hardware operates. If you are going to undertake breadboarding of a microprocessor system, a good dual trace oscilloscope with at least 15 MHz bandwidth and a logic probe are musts.

USING AN EVALUATION BOARD

If you do not wish to undertake the effort of breadboarding a microprocessor, but prefer to immediately start learning to manipulate the instruction set, an *evaluation board* is a good choice. Evaluation boards are minimal microprocessor systems supplied by the microprocessor manufacturer or an independent manufacturer. Figure 12-2 is a photograph of a typical microprocessor evaluation board using a calculator-like keyboard to enter instructions and simple LEDs for data display. A monitor routine is contained in a preprogrammed ROM.

Evaluation boards generally do not come with power supplies and you must obtain or build suitable power supplies. Evaluation boards may be purchased in either kit or assembled form. In both cases the evaluation board is somewhat more expensive than the breadboard but it has the advantage of starting with a system that works. The prices on evaluation boards range from a few hundred dollars to the $400 to $600 region. Obviously, as the price increases, so does the sophistication of the evaluation board.

A simple evaluation board has input switches, data display, and a preprogrammed monitor in ROM. Using this simple evaluation board you can manipulate a microprocessor instruction set and observe the results on the display. If you

Fig. 12-2. A microprocessor breadboard system with an 8080 microprocessor expansion socket, an octal keyboard, and an I/O expansion socket. Photo courtesy E & L Instruments.

purchase a more sophisticated evaluation board it may have provisions to connect an external terminal such as a teletypewriter. Evaluation boards permitting teletypewriter connection have a more sophisticated monitor program and, thus, allow the user to write programs considerably more extensive than those used with the simpler evaluation boards or with a breadboard system.

The very best evaluation boards have provisions for a console terminal such as a teletypewriter, for memory expansion, and for permitting the user to breadboard circuitry at the various I/O ports. Using these sophisticated evaluation boards, you can experiment with I/O addressing and microprocessor control of external devices. These sophisticated breadboards usually have provision for ROM and RAM expansion. If you are going to expand the ROM, you must have facilities to "blast" ROMs or have the ROMs "blasted" at a semiconductor distributor.

Evaluation boards are available for a great number of different microprocessors. There are numerous evaluation boards available built around the 6800 and the 8080. For this reason, almost any level of evaluation board sophistication is available using these two popular microprocessors.

USING A MICROCOMPUTER

If the computer hobbyist bug really bites, you will not be satisfied with anything less than a complete personal computer. Of course, this personal computer may be built around one of the many popular microprocessors. Nonetheless, though, it is a complete computer. Using a hobbyist computer is extremely educational and provides by far the greatest range of experimental capabilities. Hobby computers can be programmed by machine language and the detailed hardware operations of the microprocessor and its associated circuits can be observed. On the other hand, you can immediately turn to higher level languages, such as BASIC, and concentrate on sophisticated programming techniques leaving machine language and hardware for someone else. Needless to say, using a hobbyist microcomputer is considerably more expensive than using the evaluation board or a breadboard.

Figure 12-3 is a photograph of a typical hobbyist system. Although most hobbyist microcomputers may be used on a stand-alone basis, that is, without a *terminal,* by far the greatest use of the microcomputer is obtained when the microcomputer is attached to a terminal such as a video terminal or a teletypewriter. In addition to using a terminal, most microcomputers make use of some form of *mass storage* and fairly sizeable amounts of *memory expansion.*

The basic cost of a microcomputer may appear to be somewhat deceptive. The published prices for basic microcomputers are frequently less than the prices for sophisticated evaluation boards. In order to make the microcomputer operational, memory expansion is frequently

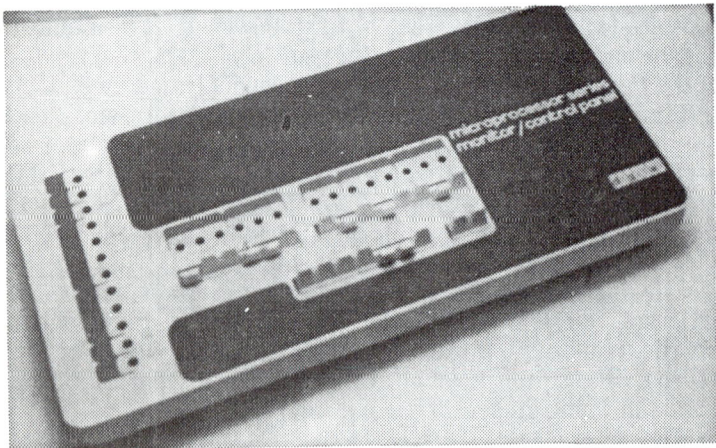

Fig. 12-3. A microcomputer built around a microprocessor. The front panel, with bit switches and bit LED readouts, is similar to a microprocessor front panel.

required, as many basic microcomputers do not offer any memory in the base price. Memory expansion normally comes in 4K increments. If you desire to operate a moderately sophisticated system, capable of higher level languages such as BASIC as well as machine language programming, approximately 12K of memory is required. Frequently the microcomputer does not include an I/O port to communicate with the terminal. Therefore, an I/O port must be purchased. Of course, the terminal and some form of mass storage must be acquired as well. By the time you have acquired a microcomputer, adequate memory, an I/O port, a terminal, and mass storage you will probably spend close to $1,000. However, for $1,000 you have a complete digital computer, capable of providing you with many hours of highly instructional entertainment, as well as providing valuable computational and control services.

Once you have obtained your microprocessor-based computer system, you will be able to experiment with machine language, text editors, assembly language, and a number of high level languages. If you are hardware oriented, you may add parallel I/O cards to your microcomputer system and literally *interface* the world. If you are software oriented, you have the capability of writing very sophisticated programs and even developing new languages, assemblers, and compilers. The microprocessor opens the door to a whole new world of hobbyist activity.

Appendix A

Powers of Two

n	2^n	2^n THREE BYTE BINARY		
0	1	00000000	00000000	00000001
1	2	00000000	00000000	00000010
2	4	00000000	00000000	00000100
3	8	00000000	00000000	00001000
4	16	00000000	00000000	00010000
5	32	00000000	00000000	00100000
6	64	00000000	00000000	01000000
7	128	00000000	00000000	10000000
8	256	00000000	00000001	00000000
9	512	00000000	00000010	00000000
10	1024	00000000	00000100	00000000
11	2048	00000000	00001000	00000000
12	4096	00000000	00010000	00000000
13	8192	00000000	00100000	00000000
14	16384	00000000	01000000	00000000
15	32768	00000000	10000000	00000000
16	65536	00000001	00000000	00000000
17	131072	00000010	00000000	00000000
18	262144	00000100	00000000	00000000
19	524288	00001000	00000000	00000000
20	1048576	00010000	00000000	00000000
21	2097152	00100000	00000000	00000000
22	4194304	01000000	00000000	00000000
23	8388608	10000000	00000000	00000000

ASCII Characters

EVEN PARITY BIT	7-BIT OCTAL CODE	CHARACTER	DESCRIPTION
0	000	NUL	NULL, TAPE FEED, CONTROL SHIFT P.
1	001	SOH	START OF HEADING; ALSO SOM, START OF MESSAGE, CONTROL A,
1	002	STX	START OF TEXT; ALSO EOA, END OF ADDRESS, CONTROL B,
0	003	ETX	END OF TEXT: ALSO EOM, END OF MESSAGE CONTROL C,
1	004	EOT	END OF TRANSMISSION (END): CONTROL D,
0	005	ENQ	ENQUIRY; ALSO WRU, CONTROL E,
0	006	ACK	ACKNOWLEDGE. ALSO RU, CONTROL F.
1	007	BEL	RINGS THE BELL. CONTROL G.
1	010	BX	BACKSPACE: ALSO FEO, FORMAT EFFECTOR. BACKSPACE SOME MACHINES, CONTROL H.
0	011	HT	HORIZONTAL TAB. CONTROL I.
0	012	LF	LINE FEED (NEW LINE): ADVANCES PAPER TO NEXT LINE, DUPLICATED BY CONTROL J.
1	013	VT	VERTICAL TAB (VTAB). CONTROL K.
0	014	FF	FORM FEED TO TOP OF NEXT PAGE (PAGE). CONTROL L.

EVEN PARITY BIT	7-BIT OCTAL CODE	CHARACTER	DESCRIPTION
1	015	CR	CARRIAGE RETURN TO BEGINNING OF LINE. DUPLICATED BY CONTROL M.
1	016	SO	SHIFT OUT: CHANGES RIBBON COLOR TO RED. CONTROL N.
0	017	SI	SHIFT IN: CHANGES RIBBON COLOR TO BLACK. CONTROL 0
1	020	DLE	DATA LINK ESCAPE. CONTROL P (DCO)
0	021	DC1	DEVICE CONTROL 1, TURNS TRANSMITTER (READER) ON, CONTROL Q (XON)
0	022	DC2	DEVICE CONTROL 2, TURNS PUNCH OR AUXILIARY ON. CONTROL R (TAPE, AUX ON).
1	023	DC3	DEVICE CONTROL E, TURNS TRANSMITTER (READER) OFF, CONTROL S (XOFF).
0	024	DC4	DEVICE CONTROL 4. TURNS PUNCH OR AUXILIARY OFF. CONTROL T (TAPE, AUX OFF)
1	025	NAK	NEGATIVE ACKNOWLEDGE: ALSO ERR. ERROR. CONTROL U.
1	026	SYN	SYNCHRONOUS IDLE (SYNC). CONTROL V.
0	027	ETB	END OF TRANSMISSION BLOCK: ALSO LEM. LOGICAL END OF MEDIUM. CONTROL W.
0	030	CAN	CANCEL (CANCL). CONROL X.
1	031	EM	END OF MEDIUM. CONTROL Y.
1	032	SUB	SUBSTITUTE. CONTROL Z.
0	033	ESC	ESCAPE. PREFIX.
1	034	FS	FILE SEPARATOR. CONTROL SHIFT L.
0	035	GS	GROUP SEPARATOR. CONTROL SHIFT M.
0	036	RS	RECORD SEPARATOR. CONTROL SHIFT N.
1	037	US	UNIT SEPARATOR. CONTROL SHIFT O.
	040	SP	SPACE.
0	041	!	
0	042	"	
1	043	#	
0	044	$	
1	045	%	
1	046	&	
0	047	'	ACUTE ACCENT OR APOSTROPHE.
0	050	(	
1	051	)	

EVEN PARITY BIT	7-BIT OCTAL CODE	CHARACTER	DESCRIPTION
1	052	*	
0	053	+	
1	054	'	
0	055	−	
0	056	.	
1	057	/	
0	060	0	
1	061	1	
1	062	2	
0	063	3	
1	064	4	
0	065	5	
0	066	6	
1	067	7	
1	070	8	
0	071	9	
0	072	:	
1	073	;	
0	074	<	
1	075	=	
1	076	>	
0	077	?	
1	100		
0	101	A	
0	102	B	
1	103	C	
0	104	D	
1	105	E	
1	106	F	
0	107	G	
0	110	H	
	111	I	
1	112	J	
0	113	K	
1	114	L	
0	115	M	
0	116	N	
1	117	O	
0	120	P	
1	121	Q	
1	122	R	
0	123	S	
1	124	T	
0	125	U	
0	126	V	

EVEN PARITY BIT	7-BIT OCTAL CODE	CHARACTER	DESCRIPTION
1	127	W	
1	130	X	
0	131	Y	
0	132	Z	
1	133	[	SHIFT K
0	134		SHIFT L
1	135	]	SHIFT M
1	136		SHIFT N
0	137	→	
0	140		ACCENT GRAVE.
0	175		THIS CODE GENERATED BY ALT MODE.
0	176		THIS CODE GENERATED BY ESC KEY (IF PRESENT)
1	177	DEL	DELETE, RUB OUT.
1	141	a	
1	142	b	
0	143	c	
1	144	d	
0	145	e	
0	146	f	
1	147	g	
1	150	h	
0	151	i	
0	152	j	
1	153	k	
0	154	l	
1	155	m	
1	156	n	
0	157	o	
1	160	p	
0	161	q	
0	162	r	
1	163	s	
0	164	t	
1	165	u	
1	166	v	
0	167	w	
0	170	x	
1	171	y	
1	172	z	
0	173		
1	174		

Index

181